Alexandra the GREAT

The Story of the Record–
Breaking Filly
Who Ruled the Racetrack

Deb Aronson

CHICAGO
REVIEW
PRESS

Copyright © 2017 by Deb Aronson
All rights reserved
Published by Chicago Review Press Incorporated
814 North Franklin Street
Chicago, Illinois 60610
ISBN 978-1-61373-645-6

Library of Congress Cataloging-in-Publication Data

Names: Aronson, Deb.
Title: Alexandra the Great : the story of the record-breaking filly who ruled
    the racetrack / Deb Aronson.
Description: Chicago, Illinois : Chicago Review Press, [2016] | Includes
    bibliographical references and index.
Identifiers: LCCN 2016026020 (print) | LCCN 2016047260 (ebook) | ISBN
    9781613736456 (cloth : alk. paper) | ISBN 9781613736463 (pdf) | ISBN
    9781613736487 (epub) | ISBN 9781613736470 (Kindle)
Subjects: LCSH: Rachel Alexandra (Race horse) | Race horses—United
    States—Biography. | Preakness Stakes. | Fillies.
Classification: LCC SF355.R33 A75 2016 (print) | LCC SF355.R33 (ebook) | DDC
    798.4/50929—dc23
LC record available at https://lccn.loc.gov/2016026020

Interior design: Sarah Olson

Printed in the United States of America
5 4 3 2 1

To my husband, Ben Williams, who is the light of my life. And to the late Jo Hooker, whose bright smile and endless enthusiasm about Rachel Alexandra made this project even more fun. She is deeply missed.

Contents

A Nobody

LOTTA KIM SWEATED AND paced restlessly in her dark stall on a late January night in 2006. Her hooves rustled the deep straw. Her baby was coming, whether she liked it or not.

At midnight Jim, the night watchman at Heaven Trees Farm in Lexington, Kentucky, walked through the foaling barn, checking on those expectant mares he couldn't see from his office. As he walked down the aisle the scent of sweet, fresh hay, with a musty undertone of manure, filled the air. When he got to Lotta Kim's stall he saw her walking around and around, and back and forth, unable to settle. She would give birth tonight.

Jim stayed with Lotta Kim, watching as she tossed her black mane. Her cinnamon-colored hide glistened with sweat. In the early, ghostly hours before the dawn, her water broke, amniotic fluid gushing onto the dry, clean straw. Then Jim called Dede McGehee, the owner of Heaven Trees Farm and a well-respected horse veterinarian. "Miss Dede, Lotta Kim is in labor," Jim told her.

If Dede had been home, she would have headed to the barn. Her pink confection of a house—complete with turrets, a room filled with a bountiful display of Kentucky Derby hats, and a chicken coop miniature of her house that she called Palais de Poulets (Poultry

Dede McGehee's all-pink home. *Deb Aronson*

Palace)—was just a short walk to her foaling barn. But Dede was on the road—heading home, but not close yet. Lotta Kim was young and healthy, and Dede did not expect any complications, so she thanked Jim and told him, "If anything changes, let me know."

Next Jim called Don Barcus, the farm manager, who joined him at the foaling barn to watch over Lotta Kim. She was a **maiden**, which meant this was her first foal. The always high-strung mare was scared and tense; she sweated and panted, her eyes wide. Normally first foals are on the small side, but this one was large, and space in the mare's birth canal was tight.

Over and over, Lotta Kim got up and paced and then lay down with a grunt in the pale-pink cinderblock stall in the dark, quiet barn. For several hours she labored painfully until, finally, with Don and Jim gently pulling on the foal's forefeet, the newborn slid onto the hay. It was a girl!

This was just one foal of hundreds born that season in the Kentucky bluegrass, the nerve center of American horse racing. It would have been impossible at that moment to imagine that this little creature, more leg and bone than muscle and heart, would grow to become a racehorse for the ages, breaking **track records** and introducing thousands of people to horse racing. In a few short years, little girls and their moms would fall in love with the filly faster than you can say "girl power."

Jim and Don cleaned out the straw, now wet and dirty, and replaced it with dry bedding. They medicated the filly's naval and watched to make sure she would begin to nurse. She nosed around Lotta Kim's belly, looking for her udder. But Lotta Kim had no milk. Often, once a foal starts nursing, the mare's milk comes in. But not this time. Instead, when the filly tried to nurse, clambering around underfoot and rooting around in sensitive, ticklish areas, Lotta Kim—furious, sore, and exhausted—almost stomped her newborn. Don and Jim rushed to protect the baby.

"Whoa, whoa, settle down now, Lotta Kim," Don called out. He and Jim grabbed her halter and led her from the stall. They tried over the next few hours to interest the mare in her new baby, leading her back into the stall several times to see if she would let the filly nurse. But Lotta Kim ignored her. Finally, they took Lotta Kim away. The mare never looked back, never once whinnied for her baby.

As soon as he had led Lotta Kim away, Don climbed the stairs in the foaling barn two at a time. The next few hours were critical for the filly. Right after a mare gives birth she makes a special "first milk," or **colostrum**. Colostrum is full of antibodies that help protect a foal from disease. Without colostrum, a foal can get seriously ill and even die. And a foal can only absorb colostrum's antibodies within the first 24 hours of its life, though sooner is better.

On the upper level of the barn Dede kept spare colostrum in a freezer. When a mare has a stillborn foal or makes extra colostrum, Dede collects and freezes it just for situations like this. Don grabbed a container and thawed the thick, sticky, bright-yellow liquid. As he fed the little creature in the quiet stall, Don admired her two white socks and her unusual **blaze**, an upside-down exclamation point.

By now Dede had arrived home. She set out to find the filly a **nurse mare**, a horse that is producing milk but has no foal or whose foal has been weaned (stopped nursing). A mare like this can nurse a foal that is not her own, if she is willing. Often mares are very willing, but not always. Dede called a nearby farm with an available nurse mare and had them deliver her that day. Time was of the essence.

Dede also called Lotta Kim's owner, Dolphus ("Dolph") Morrison. Dolph, a retired steel mill manager, bred and raced Thoroughbreds as a hobby. He loved the combination of science and art that was involved with matching one of his mares (he owned mostly mares) with a promising stallion. This latest filly was the offspring of a big, strong stallion named Medaglia d'Oro, who Dolph thought was underappreciated.

Arriving at Heaven Trees, the nurse mare's owner sedated the horse lightly, to make sure she was docile, and led her off the trailer. Dede brought the nurse mare into the foaling barn. The filly saw a short, squatty mare with some Appaloosa markings walk toward her. She smelled the Vick's VapoRub, a powerfully minty-smelling ointment, which the owner had rubbed under the mare's nose and on the foal's back to mask the

Rachel Alexandra as a baby, with her striking blaze.
Suzie Oldham

unfamiliar scent of the strange new filly. Once she drank and then excreted the nurse mare's milk, the foal would begin to smell more familiar. Dede hoped that the nurse mare, who had no foal, and the filly, whose mother had rejected her, would bond.

The mare walked into the stall and began to eat from a hay net. The foal tottered over and began to nurse, nuzzling the Appaloosa's udder. The little girl was hungry! So far so good, but was the mare going to accept the filly? Nurture her body and spirit? It was anybody's guess. The nurse mare had chosen hay over the filly at first, which was not a great sign. After the nurse mare ate, Dede **hobbled** her and sat with her and the filly in the stall.

The nurse mare did not like people and was very hard to catch once she was in the **paddock**. She hated having her face touched, according to Dede, which made it challenging to grab hold of her halter. The mare quickly got a nickname that reflected her prickly nature. Since the new filly's mom was named Lotta Kim and Dede also had Lotta Kim's half-sister, Lotta Rhythm, the nurse mare, now an honorary member of the family, became Lotta Bitch (referred to hereafter as the more polite Lotta B).

Dede moved the filly and Lotta B into one of the stalls with a special viewing window, and someone also stayed with the pair constantly. The first day was critical.

Lotta B

IT WAS NOT LOVE at first sight. Lotta B didn't warm to her adopted foal immediately. But gradually, Lotta B took the filly into her care, making sure she stayed by her side. Don and Dede could tell because when they took the filly out of the stall, Lotta B whinnied loudly and frantically as the filly moved out of sight. After that the horses were inseparable. When Lotta B grazed, the filly grazed; when Lotta B got it in her mind to run, the filly ran with her.

Later, with other foals, Lotta Kim became a better mother than she was with her firstborn, who was eventually named Rachel Alexandra, after Dolph's granddaughter. Lotta Kim tolerated her next foal—**sired**, or fathered, by Empire Maker—and she bonded strongly with her third foal, Samantha Nicole, who was named after Dolph's other granddaughter and is Rachel Alexandra's full sister (they have the same sire, Medaglia D'Oro). Lotta Kim whinnied frantically when Samantha Nicole was weaned from her. She missed her foal.

With her new mother, Rachel Alexandra had a carefree life at Heaven Trees. She romped and cavorted in the large paddock with her playmates, including Mogul Maker, whose mom was Lotta Rhythm. They raced up the hills and then back down, running along the fence and coming to the gate whenever they saw a human

Rachel Alexandra cavorting. *Suzie Oldham*

visitor who might have treats. The only time Rachel
Alexandra, Mogul Maker, and the other foals came into
the barn was to get breakfast and take a nap. There Don,
Jim, and Dede checked her and her friends over, to make
sure they had good appetites and no injuries, and then
out the foals scampered into the thrilling, rolling green
hills again.

Rachel Alexandra was big; bigger and taller than the
other foals, and not just because she was older than the
rest. In addition, Dede noticed that Rachel, even at this
young age, was good natured and smart, a pleasure to
be around, unlike her mother. When Rachel came into
the barn in the mornings, she let Dede and the others
handle her without flinching, her big brown eyes calm
and bright. It was as if Rachel knew the routine and was
happy to cooperate.

Soon it was time to wean the foals. So one morning,
while Rachel and her foal friends were in the paddock
with their mares, Dede culled Lotta B from the herd
and took her back to her own farm. Rachel whinnied
and nickered for her foster mom, but soon enough her
friends enticed her back into **galloping** and frolicking
together in the beautiful Kentucky bluegrass. Rachel
was growing up.

Even with her superior size, all that running and fresh
air, all the grass and good, nutritious grains and oats she
could eat, Rachel Alexandra was still a skinny, scruffy-
looking foal. With her big knobby knees and her muscle-
free physique, it looked as if she had not inherited those

traits that Dolph had admired in her parents. She was considered an ugly duckling whose build would make an unsuitable racehorse. It's just the luck of the draw, Dolph knew, and he prepared to sell her and Mogul Maker at a big auction.

But his plans for Rachel Alexandra were derailed. Before she could be sold, a veterinarian examined her to make sure she was healthy and sound, a requirement for all **weanlings** going to the sale. Two days before the sale, the vet called Dolph.

"Your little filly has an OCD," the vet said. OCD, osteochondritis dissecans, occurs sometimes when a young horse grows very fast. OCD can cause swelling and pain in a horse's joints and can cause little bumps or lesions, bone chips, bone cysts, or bone-on-bone wear. Since Rachel had some lesions, Dolph knew she would not earn the $125,000 he thought she was worth, and he withdrew her from the sale. Mogul Maker went to the auction block and sold for $350,000, but Dolph's profit from Rachel Alexandra would have to wait. What was he going to do with Rachel?

Diamond D

"RACHEL CAN STAY with me until you decide what to do," Dede told Dolph.

Dolph approached his racehorse hobby just like he had his steel business. The key to his success as a top executive and manager of steel mills, he believed, had been finding good people, getting out of their way, and letting them do their jobs. He hired people he trusted.

Dolph knew Dede was smart, loyal, and very good with horses, and he trusted her to do what was best for Rachel. So he agreed. Rachel didn't get sold, but she didn't get to go back to the rolling green hills of Heaven Trees Farm. Instead she joined other weanlings, including one of Dolph's other weanlings, Abbott Hall, on an extra piece of land Dede rented just down the road. The land was rolling, like at Heaven Trees, but it had no special name or pink-painted buildings—simply a few shelters and two nondescript barns. It was fine space, but it wasn't heavenly.

At Heaven Trees Dede coddled newborns and pregnant mares, as well as mares she was trying to help get pregnant. She used this other land to house horses that were in transition: infertile mares, weanlings and **yearlings** that were about to be sold, or horses that were ill. By reducing the number of horses on her farm, Dede could protect the turf at Heaven Trees from overgrazing and the pounding of too many sharp hooves.

On the land Dede rented, Rachel marked her first birthday, which for all racehorses is considered January 1, no matter what month they are born. She stayed until summer, when it was time to move onward and upward. The yearling was ready to attend racing school. Since he couldn't sell her for what she was worth, Dolph decided to go ahead and train the filly to see how she might develop.

The sun baked the Kentucky bluegrass on the brutally hot August day. Rachel Alexandra walked into the shiny horse trailer and rode 900 miles to Lone Oak, Texas, which would be her home for the next nine months.

Fifteen hours later the van stopped at Lone Oak's single traffic light, then pulled on past the gas station and the Subway, the only restaurant in town, on its way to Diamond D Ranch. Diamond D is a training center that has 185 acres, 16 paddocks, 7 pastures, 3 barns, 82 stalls, an indoor riding ring and indoor walking ring, plus a vet room, foaling stalls, and a grooming center. Diamond D had space for many more horses than Rachel's previous home.

When the van pulled up to the entrance of the ranch the large, black metal gates swung open. Despite the heat Rachel had made the trip safely and in good health. She was ready to begin the next phase of her life.

Run by Scooter Dodwell and his father, Ed (who died in 2012), Diamond D is like school for horses, except instead of learning to read, write, and do arithmetic, horses learn to race. The Dodwells harness a horse's natural desire to run so it can compete on the racetrack with a jockey perched like a flea on its back.

Scooter—and Ed before him—had trained many horses for many owners, but Dolph had been their loyal customer the longest, for 25 years. Dolph trusted them to do a good job, just like he trusted Dede.

Scooter hardly noticed the big filly's striking blaze as she tromped down the ramp and off the van. That's because he saw something else that filled his heart with dismay: Rachel had the dreaded **shark eye**. When you can see the whites of a horse's eye, the so-called shark eye, that horse is often ornery or high-strung, or both.

Scooter knew Rachel's mom well. Even without a shark eye, that Lotta Kim was a tempest. Sure she was smart, but she used those brains to be willful and ornery. She battled Scooter using her compact, strong body to resist his every command. Rachel was a big horse already, bigger than her mom.

"Are you gonna fight me like your mama did?" Scooter asked Rachel as he led her to her new stall. Rachel looked at him, ears up and swiveling around, absorbing the details of her new home, the building as long as a football field, lined with stalls. Her own stall had a window looking out onto the paddocks and race-track and had fresh alfalfa-hay bedding.

Scooter only knew Rachel as "the Lotta Kim filly" at this point, since she was not yet named. "Lotta Kim was hard enough to break," he said to Ed that evening as they did the late feeding, walking down the row of stalls in the large barn, scooping feed into each horse's bucket. "And this Lotta Kim filly has that awful shark eye on her too. This is going to be fun."

Ed just smiled and sympathized. His son didn't fool him one bit. He knew they both took pride in their oper-ation and wouldn't let a challenge like this spook them.

Diamond D uses patience and endless repetition when training its yearlings. Thoroughbred racehorses improve with structure and routine. A horse has to be shown new skills over and over again until they are no longer new but become part of the fabric of the horse's days.

The next day, early in the morning, Scooter came to Rachel's stall.

"Good morning," he said, stroking her nose and look-ing into her eyes. Rachel snorted and bobbed her head.

"Might as well get this started," he told Jésus Pérez, one of the riders who trained the young horses. Jésus entered Rachel's stall carrying a saddle. The slender, clean-cut young man was all business, but it was a business he loved. He knew, from a decade of experience, how to handle yearlings, gently yet firmly, to introduce them to the many new and strange experiences they would encounter in training, and how to prevent them from being overwhelmed.

Horse handlers call the early training process "breaking" a horse, but that term is misleading. The process involves getting a horse to tolerate a person mounting and riding it. Jésus's first goal was to introduce Rachel to the saddle by putting it on her back. He hoped she wouldn't go berserk. Often a horse will buck and twist the first time it feels a saddle on its back. It feels like a predator has jumped on its back, and its instinct is to get rid of the predator. Rachel stood calmly, looking over her shoulder to watch the action. When Jésus put a bit in her mouth, she chomped on it, feeling the hard, cold metal with her tongue and teeth. She was willing to go along with this new routine, it seemed. Many horses clamp their teeth tight so their handlers can't put a bit in their mouths, and many lift their noses up high once the bit is in, so their handlers can't reach up to fit the halter over their ears. Horses often are skittish about their ears. But not Rachel.

After wearing the saddle a little bit every day for several days, Rachel experienced driving reins. Driving reins go from the bit in the horse's mouth to the ground behind the horse. Jésus stood on the ground behind Rachel and helped her get used to the feel of the bit in her mouth and the pressure of the reins telling her when to stop or turn. How strange to go from running wild and free on the Kentucky farm to having another being control one's smallest movements. Many horses take a long time to get used to it. Rachel adapted quickly.

Next came a big step. Jésus got on Rachel's back. First he lay on his stomach so she could get used to his weight. Plus he could jump off fast if she started bucking. But Rachel did not panic. She accepted the weight gracefully.

After a couple days of that exercise, Jésus sat on her back. He used a western saddle, which is larger than a racing saddle and has a horn the rider can grab if the horse bucks or bolts. Rachel walked serenely around a pen, first in one direction and then in the other. The next day she did the same thing, and for a little longer than the day before.

Although at 16 **hands** tall (a hand is four inches) Rachel was big for her age, she was still young, so no one spent a long time on her back. After a few days walking in the pen, she was ready to ride up and down the narrow dirt lane that ran between various pastures at Diamond D. The path had fences on either side and gates every hundred yards, so even if a yearling spooked, it couldn't run too far or hurt itself. Needless to say, Rachel did not spook. Jésus rode her up and down the lane, and she acted as if she'd been carrying people on her back and obeying instructions through reins all her life.

Scooter quickly realized that Rachel's shark eye was misleading. From the beginning, Rachel Alexandra handled herself with calm and poise. Horses each have a very different personality, just like humans do. Some horses are lazy, some are anxious or nervous, some are smart, and some are not so smart. Some smart ones use their wits to avoid or resist things they don't want to do, and others use them to compete and cooperate. The true horse enthusiast understands each horse as an individual and tailors his or her treatment of the horse accordingly.

It amazed Scooter to discover that he only had to show Rachel something once for her to get it. And, unlike her mom, she was good-natured. Best of all, she loved to run.

Rachel Alexandra stood out from the moment she arrived at Diamond D Ranch. It wasn't just because of her large size, her big stride, her special blaze, her glossy coat (which had finally turned to a beautiful dark chocolate), or even her shark eye. It was because she was clearly a spirited, natural racehorse from the start.

Her second month at Diamond D, Rachel and her fellow yearlings Abbott Hall, Silver Doll, Forward Sail, Bonanza Babe, Sarah Sue, Lucky Approval, and Jetta Bug went to the track. Diamond D has its own sandy loam (a sand and clay mix) racetrack, an ideal texture for running on, that is identical to an official track. Each day Rachel trotted or jogged around the track with a rider on her back. Soon her big, heavy western saddle changed to an exercise saddle, which is still larger than the dinner-plate-sized racing saddles but smaller than a western saddle, and has no horn for the rider to grab.

Next Rachel began galloping around the track, starting out with short distances and gradually running a full mile or two. Immediately she mesmerized Ed, his wife Caroline, and Scooter. One morning, as Rachel worked out, the trio stood at the fence watching. The horse's ears were up, and her stride ate up the ground.

"Look how long her stride is and how relaxed she runs," Scooter said to his dad. "She beats every horse in the house, and she doesn't get tired, even if we run her a mile."

"You bet," Ed agreed as Rachel finished her workout. "And she looks as alert and rested as when she began."

The Dodwells knew this was a good sign that she might have what it takes to excel at the track. And Rachel wasn't even finished growing yet.

Rachel was well cared for at Diamond D. She enjoyed fresh air and sunshine every day. She ran with her buddies around the track. She dined three times a day on oats and sweet feed, with hay whenever she wanted it. Like everything else she did, Rachel excelled at eating. She never left a single oat behind in her bucket.

Now Rachel was ready for some hard work, and for the next 30 days she had a new routine: running and competing with another yearling. First they raced short distances, like 1/16 of a mile. Gradually the distance grew. Every week Scooter would call Dolph to tell him about how his horses were shaping up.

Antonio Dominguez, Rachel's regular **groom**, used a curry comb and brush on her glossy coat every morning before their work began. He knew Rachel was running fast, but he also knew there was more to racing than quickness. Rachel looked at and listened to Antonio, her eyes soft and her face relaxed. It almost seemed to him that she understood what he was saying. She seemed willing to do whatever Scooter, Jésus, and he wanted her to.

For horses, just like people, practice makes perfect. Yearlings have to learn to run in a crowd of other horses, but they also have to learn to run alone. Otherwise, when they get in the lead in a race, they'll slow down until the crowd joins them again. First Rachel practiced running on the inside of the track, with other horses on her right, and then she practiced running on the outside with other horses on her left. It didn't matter what position she was in or if her trainers ran her slow or fast; it was as if she understood the purpose of each exercise, and she easily completed each one.

By now the yearlings had earned a vacation. The last three months of work had carefully stressed their leg bones, and getting a chance to rest allowed them to heal. This stress followed by rest makes the leg bones—the most vulnerable part of any racehorse—stronger.

So the next two months Rachel lounged in the paddock and ate fresh grass with her friends while she healed. And as her bones got stronger, her muscles did too. She also appeared to miss her workouts. During her vacation, when the other yearlings grazed or horsed around, Rachel would often stand by the fence closest to the track, away from her pals, and watch the other horses work.

Rachel was clearly the fastest horse of Diamond D's crop, and she was not shy about strutting her stuff. It was as if she knew she was the best. She didn't push the other yearlings around, but she certainly did not allow them to bully her either. Already she had the demeanor and personality that set her apart from other horses, like a queen from her subjects.

Before Rachel's vacation Scooter had x-rayed her knees and ankles to make sure her bones and joints looked healthy and strong. Sometimes, especially if a horse is slow to mature or is on the young side, its bone density might be low. That can make its bones weak and more likely to break. If a horse has low bone density, Scooter recommends that the owner wait to race the horse late in the two-year-old year or even until it is three years old. That gives the horse time to mature and build stronger bones.

There's no denying that horse racing poses some risks to horses. Ruffian, the most famous filly in the world, ran faster than any other filly and never lost a race. That is, until she ran a match (one-on-one) race against the 1975 Kentucky Derby winner, Foolish Pleasure. In that race she crushed the **sesamoid bones** of her right **fetlock** (the lower part of her leg, just above and behind the hoof) so badly that her hoof was hanging limp from her leg. Ruffian had an unfortunate family history of weak bones. Her sire, Reviewer, for example, suffered three breakdowns in his racing career. After his fourth and last breakdown, which occurred while in his paddock, he had to be **euthanized**. Shenanigans, Ruffian's **dam** (her mother), also broke two legs during her life. Ruffian's **damsire** (maternal grandfather), Native Dancer, has a reputation for passing his "soft bone" genetics to his offspring.

Rachel was not related to Native Dancer and did not have that same family history. She was a big, strong filly, and her bones were magnificent. Scooter thought she had real promise and told Dolph so. He never imagined what an understatement that would prove to be.

Finally, in February, Rachel's vacation ended and she could run again. As her muscles grew stronger and her body grew bigger and fitter, she became even more energetic and was harder to control. Sometimes she just wanted to take off. *Let me run!* she seemed to say. *Let me run!*

At times while she ran Rachel couldn't resist taking the bit in her teeth, to keep it from tugging on the soft flesh of her mouth, so she could ignore Jésus when he tried to slow or stop her. But she also listened to Jésus and Scooter and learned to relax, which enabled her to run farther faster.

Running on the track came naturally to Rachel, but stepping into the starting gate is not natural for any horse. Horses feel claustrophobic the first times they are asked to enter this narrow metal stall. Once a horse is closed into the gate, it can't go forward or backward. For an animal whose first instinct when afraid is to flee, the gate feels very threatening. In addition, at the start of a race, tensions are high and gate assistants are yelling. Horses pick up on that anxiety, which ratchets up their own anxiety and tension.

The first time Jésus walked Rachel Alexandra to the gate, he had several helpers standing by. The gate was open on both ends, and Jésus led the horse slowly through it. Her ears twisted, first one way and then the other, but she didn't twitch her tail or pin her ears back. So far, so good. Next Scooter closed the front of the gate and had Rachel stand in the enclosure with the back open.

"That's a girl," he murmured to her as she lifted first one foot and then the other and looked around to see what would happen next. Next Scooter closed the back of the gate, shutting her in. She stood calmly in the small, enclosed space as if she'd done it all her life. Somehow she knew just what was needed and was willing to oblige. Rachel was one smart horse!

Once the yearlings were comfortable in the gates, they practiced starting in pairs, as if they were in a real race. By this time Rachel was the fastest of the group by far. Poor Silver Doll! Rachel beat that horse, her most regular training buddy, every race.

One morning, when the bluebonnets and other Texas wildflowers were beginning to bloom, Scooter told Rachel Alexandra, "Dolph wants to sell you, but I think I can convince him not to." Rachel tossed her head and snorted, nuzzling Scooter as he filled her feed bucket.

Now that Rachel Alexandra was trained, Dolph thought he could get about $200,000 for her. He told Scooter to get her ready for a big sale in Florida in April. But Scooter said to him, "We got a problem. We're not selling this filly, because this is the best thing I ever trained. She is really, really fast and very smart. Plus she's the type of horse who's got something after you show it to her once. They're unusual."

Dolph trusted Scooter's opinion. So instead of selling the filly at the Ocala, Florida, horse sale, Scooter sent Rachel Alexandra on a horse trailer up to Churchill Downs, in Louisville, Kentucky. Dolph's longtime trainer, Hal Wiggins, was based there. Hal would work with Rachel to see if she might win a race or two. Once again Rachel would have to leave her home and her friends. But the love and care she had received at Diamond D, as well as her hard work, had turned her into a strong and confident horse. Her talent had blossomed, and it was time for her to show the world.

Trainer Hal Wiggins.
Suzie Oldham

Before Scooter sent Rachel to Kentucky, he decided to spare her new trainer the kind of worry he had felt when he first saw her, so he called Hal and told him, "This filly is fast. When we ship her, don't you worry about her white eye."

Rocky Start

RACHEL ALEXANDRA strolled down the horse trailer ramp in the predawn darkness. She lifted her head, arching her neck, and calmly looked around the **shedrow**, the rows of stalls facing out into the fresh air. She pawed the ground, her hoof scraping the asphalt with a sharp, grating sound.

She placidly followed Brett McLellan, Hal's assistant trainer, into stall number 16, one stall away from the office. Typically the stall right next to the office is reserved for the barn's star, its best racehorse. No one was betting on Rachel Alexandra yet though. She would have to earn that stall.

Rachel settled in. She nosed the wheat-straw bedding, so different from the wood shavings at Diamond

D, and watched as other horses were led past her stall and grooms and stable hands carried buckets and saddles to and fro along the shedrow.

Hal looked her over as he had so many of Dolph's horses. She was a good-looking, big filly. Even though she wasn't full grown, her strong back end suggested she would have plenty of power. But Hal knew that a lot of what made a good racehorse was not visible at first glance. He would get her on the track and watch her run. Sometimes it took several races to see what a horse was made of.

As a boy Hal had helped his father train a horse in the grassy area where the street ended near their small home in Port Arthur, Texas. As soon as Hal got home from school, he would saddle the horse, Allie Whit. By the time she was ready to ride, Hal's father was home from work. He would give Hal a leg up on Allie Whit, and Hal would trot her toward the open space. At Hal's father's signal, the horse would gallop fast back toward the house. Hal could feel the horse's muscles bunching and stretching beneath him and the air whooshing past him. He was flying.

Hal had been training Dolph's horses for 30 years, the last 16 of those years at Churchill Downs. He'd had a satisfying career. He had trained some good horses, though no truly spectacular ones—none that made newspaper headlines. Sure, he dreamed of hitting it big, but that was not what motivated him. For Hal, as for so many trainers, being around these magnificent creatures was not a job but a way of life and a privilege.

"The big filly looks good and strong," Hal said to Brett a few weeks after Rachel had arrived. "Let's see what she'll do in a race."

Since arriving at Churchill Downs, Rachel Alexandra had had several workouts, both long, easy gallops and shorter, faster, slightly more intense timed workouts called **breezes**. She did not slow down or struggle at the ends of these runs, and Hal decided she was ready to go.

Thoroughbred racing is measured in **furlongs**. One furlong is one-eighth of a mile, or 220 yards, so four furlongs is a half mile. A fast horse might run four furlongs in about 49 or 50 seconds. When she was older and fully grown, she would be allowed to race eight or nine furlongs, but not today. Rachel's first race would be against other two-year-old fillies—those were the rules: two-year-olds race other two-year-olds—and just 4½ furlongs. At Diamond D Rachel had breezed four furlongs at least two or three times, so Hal knew she could go the distance.

Rachel Alexandra's jockey, Brian Hernandez Jr., guided her to the gate. She had been in the gate many times at Diamond D. She knew just what to do.

The bell rang, and the gates clanged open. Rachel broke fast, but she couldn't get the lead. Coming to the turn, she was fifth. The horses ahead of her kicked dirt and sand in her face. Rachel stumbled as other horses bumped into her. Her stride was short and choppy. Brian tried, but he couldn't help Rachel get around the other horses to run with the long strides Hal had seen her use. She finished sixth out of nine fillies, and when she got to the finish line, she just kept running. She apparently didn't feel tired at all, and Brian had to pull hard on the reins and stand up in his stirrups to get her to slow down.

Brett's shoulders slumped. In all the years he and Hal had been working with Diamond D, Scooter had *never* sent a horse up with any kind of comment. So when Scooter said Rachel was the real deal, Brett had hoped she would come out of her first race blazing.

The horseracing industry's daily newspaper the *Daily Racing Form* reported that her performance was "no menace, inside."

Hal's wife, Renée, was at the races that day. After that race she turned to Hal with a look on her face as if to say, *You big dummy.*

"You've been telling me ever since she arrived that Rachel was probably the best horse you've ever trained? You have got to be kidding me," she said in her Texas twang.

"Well, it's true. I'd hoped she'd place better than that," Hal admitted, but he tried not to fret. Training horses is as much an art as a science, and if trainers worry too much, they just end up with ulcers. "But did you see the energy she had after the finish?" he asked Renée. "When the race was over she just took off, running past everybody, her ears straight up. You could see how much energy she had left over. I think she has the stamina to be a truly fine racer."

Stamina is at least as important as speed in racing. Dolph believed stamina was key and tried to breed it into every horse. To do that he looked for horses with "good airways." Medaglia d'Oro, Rachel's sire, had an outstanding airway. Usually as a horse matures, its stamina increases, just as its bones and muscles strengthen. It looked like Rachel already had the stamina of a winner.

Hal wasn't worried that Rachel didn't win. Not many horses have won every race they've ever run. No matter how much training it has had, a horse is still learning a new routine in the first race or two. There is even a term for horses that have not won a race—**maidens**. When a horse wins its first race, racing pros say it "broke its maiden." It took Seabiscuit, the famous horse who outran the bigger, stronger War Admiral, 17 races to break his maiden.

Hal entered Rachel Alexandra in a second race for two-year-old fillies. The race was scheduled for Friday, June 13, three weeks after her first race. Could that be Rachel's lucky day? The day she would break her maiden?

Once again there were nine fillies lined up for the race. Rachel Alexandra was one smart horse. Scooter always said, "You show her something once, and she gets it." This time she got it; she catapulted out of the gate and grabbed the lead so commandingly that it was as if her gate opened before all the rest.

She seemed to like being in the lead! She could stretch out and go, without dirt and sand being kicked into her face, without other horses bumping into her.

Renée and her friend Jo Hooker were at the racetrack that day. "Who is *that?*" Jo asked when she saw a horse leap into the lead.

"That's us!" Renée exclaimed, and Jo grabbed her arm and jumped up and down.

Rachel led, just like the famous filly Ruffian always did, for the whole race. Near the final furlong Best Lass ranged up next to Rachel Alexandra, challenging her, but Rachel sped up a little more and Best Lass dropped back, spent.

Friday the 13th was indeed Rachel's lucky day. She won her first race!

Rachel was a fast learner. During her first race she earned what is called a Beyer speed figure of 51. During the second race, her Beyer speed figure was 85. Pretty good for a beginner. (The Beyer speed figure compares horses' performances at different tracks at different times. It helps people who are betting know which horse is most likely to win. Top racehorses can earn numbers in the 100s. Groovy, the 1987 American Champion Sprint Horse, earned the highest figure ever of 134.)

Two weeks later Hal entered Rachel Alexandra in the Debutante Stakes, also at Churchill Downs. It was a strong field of young fillies, but Hal knew Rachel could win. For Rachel it was no different from the other two races, even though the prize money, or **purse**, was much larger, at $100,000. Rachel, led by Brett and her groom, Rubin Flores, joined the parade of horses around the dirt track to the **saddling paddock**.

The gates opened, and Rachel bounced away. Even as she was finding her rhythm, however, she bumped into a couple other horses. She couldn't seem to find the right gear. Once again she got squeezed by a group of horses, and Brian couldn't guide her out. Finally Rachel found her stride and put on a very strong late burst, catching all but one horse. She had to settle for second.

Hal told Brett not to fret. "Did you see how she drew off real easy at the end, as if she had a whole extra race in her? She's a good 'un," Hal assured his assistant.

Even though she didn't win that important race, other owners and trainers noticed that Rachel Alexandra looked really good racing. Aside from being big for a filly, with strong hindquarters, she had an exceptionally long stride. For every two strides she took, many horses had to take three or even four. That meant she could go longer and farther since she took fewer strides to cover the same distance. People started to pay attention.

International Equine Acquisitions Holdings, Inc. (IEAH), a large Thoroughbred racing company based in Lexington, noticed, for example. That July they offered to buy Rachel Alexandra from Dolph's small operation for $1.2 million, and Dolph was ready to sell her. However, when a vet examined Rachel, he found a small chip in her ankle, and IEAH withdrew its offer.

Who knows how Rachel's story might have unfolded if she had been sold? Would IEAH have uncovered and fully tapped her potential? Would Rachel ever have been teamed up with the jockey who rode her to fame and fortune? Those questions can never be answered, but what's clear is that, for many of the people involved in training and caring for her, Rachel's injury would turn out to be a blessing in disguise.

A bone chip is easily removed with a routine surgery that requires only a very small incision. Still, Rachel could not race for four months after the procedure. She had to stay in her stall for the first 10 days, coming out only once a day, for a bath. Then for six weeks she was **handwalked** around the shedrow for just a half hour each day.

"Many horses would be half silly, wanting to jump around," said Hal to Brett.

Finally, Rachel was allowed to go to the track and trot for four or five days. Later she was allowed to gallop and then, eventually, to breeze. It was a long road back, but she was ready to go by early October, so Hal entered her in a mid-October race at Keeneland Racecourse in Lexington, Kentucky.

The morning of the race, Brett led her into the saddling paddock. When a horse is being trained, it gets saddled in its stall. On race day, it is led to a separate enclosure, the saddling paddock, with all the other horses entered in that race. The public can watch all the horses while they are being saddled, see how they are behaving, and watch the jockeys mount and walk the horses to the starting gates. It's a chance to see the beautiful horses up close.

As she entered the saddling paddock, Rachel's ears pricked up, her feet got bouncy, her body began to vibrate. She had her party feet on! "The only thing that gets Rachel Alexandra excited is letting her race," Hal joked to Brett.

Rachel's **track pony**—a quarter horse ridden alongside a racehorse to keep the racehorse calm and steady
while not racing—did not appreciate her high spirits, but
Dolph and his wife, Ellen, and Hal and Renée grinned.
Their girl loved to run, and she was ready to go.

Brian was just a passenger that day. Rachel got a good
start and ran in third place for much of the race. At the
turn, she picked up speed. By the last furlong she bran-
dished even more speed, and the other horses around
her just faded away. "Anyone can ride that horse," Brian
told Brett when he hopped off after the race.

But two weeks later Rachel Alexandra came in second at the Pocahontas Stakes at Churchill, a race she
should have won. She had gotten boxed in by three other
horses and couldn't get around them until the far turn.
She shouldered her way through the crowd then as the
horses spread out a bit at the turn. But Sara Louise, running on the outside, caught the entire field, and Rachel
Alexandra ran out of racetrack before she could catch
her. Once again Rachel's ears were pricked up high and
bright at the end of the race, which hadn't tired her in
the least.

Meanwhile, Dolph was having some cash-flow prob-
lems, so he decided to find a partner to invest in Rachel
Alexandra. IEAH had been interested in partnering
with him, but he did not want to be part of such a big
conglomerate. Then one day he got a call from Mike
Lauffer, a fellow Thoroughbred breeder and owner who
had seen Rachel and was interested in investing in her.

The two breeders chatted for a few minutes, and Dolph knew almost immediately that he and Mike would be good partners. He told Mike, "I'm looking to sell half of Rachel Alexandra for $600,000."

"I'll give you $500,000," Mike answered.

"It's a deal," Dolph said. "Here are the terms: I get to make every decision regarding the horse."

Mike said that sounded good to him.

It was the only time Dolph ever took on a partner.

Calvin on Board

RIDING A RACEHORSE is nothing like driving a race-car. Horses have feelings and emotions that a really good jockey can tap into and harness. In those cases, the relationship between the jockey and the horse is a powerful thing. In the story of Seabiscuit, the horse and his jockey, Red Pollard, had a special chemistry. They knew how to treat one another. Because of that chemistry, Seabiscuit became a legend.

But sometimes a horse and jockey just do not click, which can stifle a racehorse's potential. Hal and Dolph began to feel that perhaps Brian was not the best rider for Rachel, that perhaps a different jockey might unlock that extra gear Hal thought she had. At the same time,

Brian's hectic schedule was making it difficult for him to ride for Hal.

Meanwhile, the 42-year-old jockey Calvin Borel had come home from the Pocahontas Stakes and told his wife, Lisa, about this impressive horse he had seen, Rachel Alexandra.

"She looks like an incredible filly," he told Lisa. "She just got in a bad spot and couldn't get out. She couldn't get any running room."

He could tell she had enormous promise, and he wanted to find out what would happen if she got more room to run. Maybe he could be the one to help her achieve her potential.

"I'm going to get on that filly," he told Lisa.

Calvin knew horses. He grew up on his family's sugarcane farm in Catahoula Parish, in the bayou regions of southern Louisiana—an area known for producing top jockeys. Like many others in the area, the Borels were Cajun (descendants of French-speaking Canadians). The last of five boys, Calvin helped his family train their quarter horses. He had been racing horses since he was eight, when he rode on the unofficial racetracks in rural Louisiana. He won his first official race at Delta Downs in Louisiana when he was 16.

The stars aligned, and Calvin went over to Hal's barn the next day to see if he could get on that filly, just when Hal began looking for another jockey. Brian's busy schedule meant he was not going to be able to ride Rachel in her next race.

Jockey Calvin Borel.
Suzie Oldham

Calvin was like Hal: he'd had a satisfying career—he had even won the Kentucky Derby, horseracing's most famous and prestigious contest, on Street Sense two years earlier—but not a star-studded one.

The next morning he came to the stable at dawn, ready to breeze Rachel. The filly's groom, Rubin, **tacked** her up while Calvin stood by her head, caressing her nose and whispering to her.

"Hey there, sweetie," he said. "Let's see what you can do out there this morning, OK?"

Rachel allowed Calvin to stroke her, but she watched him with her shark eye, taking his measure.

"Breeze her five furlongs, Calvin," Hal told him.

"Yes, sir, Mr. Hal."

Rachel waited while Calvin hopped aboard and then took him to the far side of the track, which was shrouded in early-morning mist. Calvin reveled in the feel of her sleek muscles and long stride.

"OK, big mama," said Calvin, patting her strong neck, "let's see what you can do." With that he urged her to a gallop, warming up her muscles and loosening up her stride.

Rachel was approaching the ⅝ pole. Green-and-white poles are placed along the left border of a racetrack to signal to jockeys exactly where they are on the course. Each furlong (⅛ mile) is marked by a pole. The poles count furlongs back from the finish line, so the last pole before the finish is the ⅛ pole, the second-to-last is the ⅖ pole, and so on. When jockeys see the ⅝ pole, they know they are five furlongs from the finish, no matter how long the race is.

Now, just before reaching the ⅝ pole, Calvin angled Rachel toward the rail, loosened the reins, and urged her forward into a fast breeze. He couldn't believe how far she could travel with each thrust of her legs. It felt like she skimmed the surface of the track; Calvin could barely feel her feet touch the ground.

As Calvin and Rachel walked off the track, Calvin caught the eye of his agent, Jerry Hissam, with a look that said, *I want this horse.* It was Jerry's job to help Calvin contact trainers and get jobs riding their racehorses and to handle the contract negotiations. Jerry had been around for so long he was friends with almost all the trainers at Churchill Downs and other racetracks.

"Looks like he likes your filly," Jerry said to Hal with a laugh.

"Mr. Hal," Calvin said back at the barn, "I'd like to ride your filly. She sure does have a mighty stride."

Calvin patting Rachel. *Suzie Oldham*

"That works for me, Calvin," Hal answered. "We're booked for the Golden Rod in two weeks."

That night at home Calvin told Lisa, "I just worked the best horse I ever sat on in my life."

Lisa had heard Calvin say that before, so she didn't pay much attention. She would wait to see how the horse performed in the next race.

The day of the Golden Rod, Brett teased his friend and fellow assistant trainer Scott Blasi, "You better bring a bucket of warm water after the race." Scott's horse, War Echo, was entered in the Golden Rod Stakes as well. "You'll be cleaning off War Echo's nice white blaze once Rachel Alexandra gets done kicking dirt in her face."

Scott shook his head and laughed. He knew Brett was taunting him. That's what friends do. Brett was talking trash because he was nervous. He was trying to convince himself that Rachel Alexandra would win. Many things concerned Brett. First, Rachel was racing with Calvin for the first time. Would she run well for him? Would they click?

Second, the Golden Rod was 8½ furlongs and would be the first time Rachel would race around two turns. The farthest she had run was one mile, or eight furlongs. There were two questions on Brett's—and everyone's— mind: Could she keep her speed for the extra half furlong (110 yards)? And, more important, how would she handle having to race around two turns instead of only one? Turns were where horses risked going wide, adding distance to their race and potentially letting other horses get inside near the fence, the shortest distance around the track. The first turn would come up sooner in the race than in any other she had run. How well would Rachel manage the turns? Plus, Rachel would start in front of the grandstand, with all the noise of the crowd, not in the quieter **back stretch**.

Well, they would have their answers soon enough, Brett thought as he led her to the saddling paddock and then watched the track pony escort Rachel Alexandra and Calvin to the starting gates. One thing Brett knew: Rachel wouldn't act up in the gate. She was too smart for that nonsense.

Rachel took one, two, three big, deep breaths and stepped into the gate.

Clang! Metal on metal, the gates banged open and the horses took off. Rachel's breath exploded from her lungs as she catapulted from the gate. Running neck and neck with War Echo, her long tail flowed almost horizontally. At the first turn Rachel moved in front of War Echo, gradually stretching out along the rail until she led by 2½ lengths. Soon War Echo moved up again. As she drew even with Rachel, War Echo's jockey, Shaun Bridgmohan, saw Rachel's white eye. *Whoa!* he thought. *That horse looks crazy.* War Echo felt her jockey hesitate. They dropped back.

Around the far turn Sara Louise, who had beat Rachel in the Pocahontas Stakes, found some fresh speed. She was catching Rachel Alexandra! Calvin urged Rachel harder. "Let's go, big mama!" he yelled in his Louisiana bayou accent, thick as a good gumbo, and she leaped forward, finding another, higher gear.

"This leader is finding more," the announcer yelled. "Rachel Alexandra and Calvin Borel! And they have now slipped the field and gone clear."

The other horses simply dropped away, dusty and undistinguished, while Rachel, with her shiny dark-chocolate coat and her two white socks, shot forward and away, slipping the field, finishing five lengths ahead of the rest.

"It is Rachel Alexandra, how impressive!" the commentator continued. "Rachel Alexandra wins. Really, was there a second?"

Rachel had broken the stakes record for the Golden Rod—and she made it look easy. Trotting back toward the winner's circle, she was hardly winded. Her ears stood relaxed but at attention, her eyes were bright, and her feet were lively. She looked ready to run the race again. What a day! What a race!

Calvin, dressed in Dolph's white silks, which had a large green *D* on the torso, hopped off Rachel's back with a grin so wide he could toss it over his shoulder.

"Way to go, big mama!" he exclaimed, patting the filly's neck as they reached the winner's circle.

I was right, he thought. *This girl knew how to run.* And now Lisa was paying attention.

"When he won the Golden Rod, then we knew she was real," she said.

Calvin knew horses. He had won almost 5,000 races on some "good, good horses," but this filly, he thought, she was one for the ages. He would do everything he could from then on to stay with Rachel Alexandra.

In the winner's circle Rachel accepted the pats and the congratulations of everyone around her, from Hal and Brett to Dolph and Ellen. She acted as if this huge win were nothing special, that she had been doing this well all her life.

Brett walked Rachel back to the barn area together with the **hotwalker**. In charge of cooling a horse down after it races, the hotwalker will first walk it around and then put a blanket on it to prevent chills. Calvin grabbed his saddle to go on to his next race and then, together with Hal, walked back through the tunnel to the saddling paddock. There Hal saw John Asher, a friend and colleague who worked at Churchill Downs.

"If your filly runs like that, she could win the Oaks next year," John told him.

The Kentucky Oaks is a filly race held the day before the Kentucky Derby, which is the first of the three **Triple Crown** races. The most important events in horseracing, the Triple Crown races are run within six weeks of one another and at increasingly great distances. While the Oaks is not widely known among the general public, among racing folks, it is almost as prestigious as the Derby.

Hal appreciated John's praise but laughed and shrugged it off, knowing John was just being friendly. Hal had had a good career, but winning something like the Oaks? There is no place for dreams like that in a busy shedrow. Horses need to be trained, groomed, and fed. Bills need to be paid. Hal would continue doing as he had always done and leave others to build their castles in the sky.

But Rachel Alexandra had won the Golden Rod by such a big margin and with such a fast time that racing fans began paying attention to her. Fans liked the look of the big, strong, glossy filly. They liked the regal way she held her head high and the knowing expression in her eyes. No nervous sweating or frothing at the mouth for her. No prancing, high stepping, or fussing with the track pony chaperoning her to the gate.

Sometimes, though, she looked *so* relaxed heading to the gates that fans didn't think she had enough energy to run well. Hal encouraged his friends to bet on Rachel Alexandra, but when they saw her sudued energy, they often decided not to. They probably regretted that!

When Churchill Downs closed for the season, at the end of November, Rachel Alexandra, together with the other horses in Hal's barn, headed south to Hot Springs, Arkansas, home of the Oaklawn track. Here she would train over the winter months, but not as hard as she had during the fall.

At Oaklawn Rachel descended the trailer ramp and sauntered into her new stall. Many racehorses become uneasy and anxious when they travel. Unfamiliar sights, sounds, and smells can make them tense. But the new Oaklawn track didn't appear to faze Rachel. Sure, the shedrow was in a different place and the hay smelled a little different, but these things didn't bother her. She ate all her food and walked graciously with her groom, not fussing with him or trying to nip him, and she didn't work up a nervous sweat like some other horses did.

Every morning, when she heard Hal's car pull up in the predawn darkness, Rachel poked her head out of her stall and graciously took the peppermint he offered. After she let Hal rub her nose, Hal would head to the track kitchen for breakfast. He saw that Rachel did not mind being at a new track one little bit.

February 15, the date of the mile-long Martha Washington race at Oaklawn, seemed like a good time to start Rachel's 2009 season. She was now three years old and had grown over the winter. Sometimes when horses have a growth spurt they end up with buckled shins or just awkward and uncoordinated, like their legs are so long they could trip over them. But Rachel experienced none of that. She just kept getting better and better.

Still, Hal worried. He knew she wasn't in top form since he had trained her only lightly through the winter. She had galloped every few days but rarely, if ever, breezed since before the Golden Rod. This race would be a warm-up, he figured. And then they would see if this filly could live up to the promise she showed at the Golden Rod.

The Martha Washington

HAL TRIED HARD TO remain calm, but this filly made his heart beat faster—she was so full of promise. Unlike Hal, Rachel didn't fret. The day of the Martha Washington Stakes arrived. With Calvin on her back, Rachel sauntered out to the gate completely relaxed, and stepped inside.

"They're off!" the announcer yelled.

Rachel did not take the lead as she had at the Golden Rod, but she kept her stride long and fluid. She did not have to barrel to the front and lead all the way, as the famous filly Ruffian did. She was able to sit behind the leaders until she was ready to make her move. After the first quarter mile, only Affirmed Truth was still ahead of her. Calvin tucked Rachel in behind Affirmed Truth for the next quarter mile, pulling down his outer pair of goggles just before the turn. Calvin—like most other jockeys—always layers at least six pairs of goggles so when the first gets mud-covered, he peels them off and can see again.

At the far turn Rachel turned on her rocket power. Passing on the outside, she blew past Affirmed Truth, the fence posts along the track a blur. At the straight-away, Rachel was three lengths ahead. As her pursuers ran out of gas, Rachel was just getting started. She led by seven lengths at the finish.

Some thought the Golden Rod might have been a fluke, but after Rachel Alexandra won by seven lengths at the Martha Washington, she gained an even more devoted following. More and more fans came by the barn to take her picture and chat with Hal about her races.

Rachel didn't mind at all. She was like Secretariat, who always held a pose when someone was taking his picture. Rachel held her head high, and her big brown eyes gazed calmly at all her fans.

Rachel was looking so great on the track that Hal finally allowed himself to get excited. Maybe this was the horse he had dreamed of, the one that would take him to the very top: the big money, the big recognition. To do that with a filly, though, one has to race her against male horses—colts and geldings.

The racing public loves to watch fillies challenge the boys. But opinions are divided between those trainers, owners, and vets who find no reason *not* to race fillies with males and those who think the practice is preposterous. There are some physical differences between male and female horses, just like between male and female humans. In some sports, like sailing or bowling, physical strength is not as much of a factor, and men and women can compete on the same playing field. But in others, such as track and field, football, or ice hockey, the physical differences between genders can make it harder for women to compete against men.

Sports, or races, among horses are a similar situation. In quarter-horse races, all horses compete together, but the races are only a quarter mile (two furlongs) long—or even shorter—instead of a mile or more, as in Thoroughbred racing. In European Thoroughbred racing, the two genders race together. Fillies have been successful there. But in the United States, where there are many all-filly races, why would an owner put his or her filly up against colts?

There are examples of fillies that have beaten the boys, including Genuine Risk (who won the 1980 Kentucky Derby and was second in the Preakness Stakes, the second leg of the Triple Crown) and Winning Colors (who won the 1988 Kentucky Derby and was third in the Preakness), but sometimes those stories are high-profile tragedies, like Ruffian and Eight Belles, both of whom broke down while racing males. Usually fans remember the tragedies rather than the victories.

Ruffian, a big black filly, hadn't lost a race. She had never even been behind in a race. But she never challenged the boys, at least not until her ill-fated match race with Derby winner Foolish Pleasure in 1975. This race pitted the best filly against the best colt of the year. More than 50,000 people came to Belmont Park to watch, and twenty million people watched on television.

In 1975 women were fighting for equality. They were joining the workforce in record numbers, and feminism was strong. *Ms.* magazine had been started just a few years earlier. The battle of the sexes was in full force. So here was the match race, just like the famous tennis match between pros Billie Jean King and Bobby Riggs in 1973 that pitted a female against a male.

Three furlongs into the race, Ruffian was leading by a head when the sesamoid bones in her right fore-leg snapped. Her jockey, Jacinto Vasquez, pulled hard on her reins to get her to stop running, but Ruffian refused. She pulverized her sesamoid bones, ripped the skin of her fetlock—the region just above her hoof—and tore her ligaments. Her hoof flopped uselessly, and still she didn't stop; she tried to finish the race.

The stands were as quiet as a graveyard. Fifty thousand people were praying for the filly. Veterinarians rushed to her side. They operated on Ruffian immediately to try to save her, but she woke up from anesthesia terrified, disoriented, and thrashing her legs. In all that chaos she broke another bone. Ruffian's owners tearfully decided to euthanize her. The country's heart broke.

In 2008, the year Rachel began racing, Eight Belles came in second to Big Brown in the Kentucky Derby.

She was only the 40th filly to enter the Derby in the race's 133-year history. At the time the Democratic presidential primary was being contested, and voters were equally passionate about candidates Barack Obama and Hillary Clinton. The Derby became a proxy for their votes, with Obama fans rooting for Big Brown and Clinton fans rooting for Eight Belles. Because of that parallel, interest in the Derby was even higher than usual.

Just after the finish Eight Belles shattered bones in both her ankles so badly that she had to be euthanized at the track in front of the spectators.

Despite these tragedies, Hal began to consider entering Rachel Alexandra in a race against colts. Rachel did not come from one of the **bloodlines** that had notoriously weak leg bones. She was a strong, large, muscular filly who had been carefully trained. He believed she would not be at risk, or at least no more risk than most horses.

But he ran into a brick wall. Dolph was absolutely, positively opposed. There was no way that any filly of his was going to race against colts, risking injury or worse. For what? Glory? Prestige? Dolph did not give a fig for any of that. Rachel would race only other fillies, and that was final.

This mindset is not uncommon in Thoroughbred racing. Horse racing, traditionally, has been a male pursuit. Most trainers and breeders are men; for the most part male horses race; male jockeys ride them. In the past, only men bet on horses. Betting was not considered ladylike.

Today there are more women involved in horse racing. Rachel Alexandra's vet, Dede, is a good example,
but Dede had to fight hard to become a racehorse veterinarian, especially against her parents, who expected
her to get married and run a household, not have a pro-
fession. Female exercise riders, who work the horses
in the mornings, are common, but there are far fewer
female jockeys. One of the most successful female jockeys, Rosie Napravnik, competed in the 2011 Kentucky
Derby and won the Kentucky Oaks twice, in 2012 and
2014. Every year between 2011 and 2014, she was in the
top 10 highest-earning jockeys in North America.

Times have changed, but not entirely. Women in
horse racing are still in the minority, and in the United
States racing a filly against colts is seen as potentially
dangerous. Dolph, like many filly owners, was more
interested in protecting his horse's health than challenging his sport's traditions.

So Hal set his sights on the Kentucky Oaks, the very
race his friend John Asher had predicted Rachel could
win and Hal had dismissed as a pipe dream.

But before she ran in the Kentucky Oaks, Rachel
headed to New Orleans for the Fair Grounds Oaks. She
was, once again, at an unfamiliar track. She had already
proven that a new track, with its new sights, sounds, and
smells, did not spook her. But it had rained off and on for
several days. The track was sloppy and muddy. Rachel
had never raced on a wet track. Horses can struggle to
grip the ground when the track is wet.

Dolph checked her feet in the barn; he thought she was moving funny and wanted to make sure her shoes were on properly. In the saddling paddock Hal talked to Calvin about the track.

"I think you should take her out to the front so she doesn't get so splattered with mud," he told Calvin. "Yes, sir, Mr. Hal," Calvin said. It was the only time Hal ever told Calvin how to ride Rachel.

Many of the fillies were prancing and pulling as they came into the gate, so full of nerves they couldn't be still. Rachel took her customary three big breaths, stepped into the gate calmly, and then, when it was time, leaped out as if she'd been stung by a bee. She had a turbo-charged launch, taking three strides that exploded with power. Then, like an airplane that reaches cruising altitude, she settled into her race pace. Her message to Calvin was *You are the passenger; I am the pilot.* Calvin was smart enough to let her lead.

Rachel was ahead after the first turn, and it looked as if she would win the $400,000 stakes easily. But Calvin's hubris almost spelled disaster. One hundred yards from the finish, the jockey began to ease Rachel off, thinking they had clinched a win. One hundred yards is the length of a football field; there's still plenty of distance and time for a horse to catch the frontrunner. Rachel and Calvin were seven lengths ahead of the next horse, Flying Spur, when Calvin stood up in his stirrups, looked up to the grandstands, his face and hands covered in mud, and began shaking his finger, making the universal *We're number one* gesture. Meanwhile, Flying Spur was coming on strong, and it looked like she might catch them. Luckily for Calvin, Rachel kept running, winning by two lengths.

Calvin hopped off Rachel's back and turned to Hal.

"Boss, I don't know what she'd do if I ever asked her to run," he said. He never had to tell her to run or go faster; she just did. "She is a jockey's dream."

Another victory! But Dolph was furious. Not only was that kind of grandstanding unprofessional, he felt, but Rachel could have been hurt and Calvin could have been thrown.

"That was inexcusable," Dolph fumed to Hal.

"Yes, sir, it sure was," Hal agreed. "I'll talk to Calvin if you like."

Brett was furious too. "Let's just get another jockey," he griped to Hal. "There are plenty of jockeys who would ride a horse like Rachel without acting like an idiot."

But Hal, in his quiet, kind way, told Brett to calm down. He saw that Calvin and Rachel had a powerful bond. She ran her best with Calvin on her back, and Calvin let her tell him what to do.

Meanwhile, instead of going out to the winner's circle, everyone gathered in the tunnel between the racecourse and the saddling paddock to stay out of the rain. More than 50 people surrounded Rachel during the ceremony on that gray day: Hal, Renée, Dolph, Ellen, Calvin, Rubin, and all their friends and relations. Fans were hanging over from the stairway above, draping themselves over the railings, trying to get a glimpse of Rachel and take her picture. Blinding camera flashes went off from every direction, people were yelling themselves hoarse: "Hey, Rachel!" "Way to go, Rachel!" In such tight, noisy quarters, many horses would have bucked and kicked in fear and panic. But Rachel stood calmly and nosed Dolph on the shoulder. Maybe it was her way of saying, *Here we are. Let's enjoy ourselves.*

Rachel had a strong following now, with fans flocking to take photos of her even as Hal loaded her on the van for her trip back to Hot Springs.

"She could run on asphalt; she could run on anything," Calvin told her fans.

Spirits were high, though they narrowly escaped an embarrassing loss, and Hal had to have a talk with Calvin about his lapse in judgment on the racecourse. When they got back to Hot Springs, he summoned Calvin to meet with him at the track kitchen.

"Calvin, we were all concerned by your ride at the Martha Washington," he began, looking right in Calvin's eyes. "There at the end, when you were slowing her down, all your weight was over to one side. That's all it takes for her to take one bad step, you know."

"Oh yeah, you're right. OK, boss, I'll be more careful," Calvin said.

The two men drained their coffee and stood up. They shook hands.

"OK, then. Let's get back to work," said Hal.

Next up was the 1¹⁄₁₆-mile Fantasy Stakes at Hot Springs' Oaklawn Park. Rachel had already been so successful that other trainers were sorry she was entered.

Larry Jones, who trained Jest Jenda, knew what he was up against. "I'm afraid we're going to look like a NASCAR race here, because I'm going to just draft behind Rachel Alexandra, and maybe just settle for second," he said. (Drafting refers to riding behind another racer so the lead racer breaks the wind resistance and the racer behind doesn't have to work as hard.) "I don't know that she can be beat," he added.

Rachel seemed a little tired when she arrived at Hot Springs. Hal thought probably all the trailering, not to mention the race, might have worn her out a bit. So he gave her a few extra days off. He thought that brightened her up nicely. She had bulked up a bit too, which pleased him.

During the workout before the race, Rachel ran a half mile in 47.60 seconds, which was the fastest workout at that distance that day. She was ready. The day of the race she was heavily favored to win, and it was really no contest. The queen dominated the $150,000 race from the start, leading by almost nine lengths at the finish. Hal was very pleased.

He had meant this race to be a warm-up for the Kentucky Oaks, which would be in a month. Calvin had a different plan. Since the Oaks would be ¹⁄₁₆ mile longer than the Fantasy, he wanted to see how Rachel would do going that extra half furlong. So at the finish of the Fantasy, Calvin tapped Rachel on the shoulder to let her know she could keep running if she wanted. She took off for another furlong. The track clocker, Jim Hamilton, clocked her at 11 seconds for that last furlong. A horse doing 12 or 13 seconds at the very end of an actual race would be considered going strong. Never in his 40 years of clocking horses had Jim seen such a thing, he told Calvin. This filly had untapped reserves that no one had seen yet. Where was the bottom of Rachel's talent and speed?

Next up was the Kentucky Oaks.

Trainers, exercise riders, grooms, and jockeys do more before lunch than most people do all day. In an industry that is all about hard work day in and day out, Calvin had a reputation of being one of the hardest-working jockeys out there. Horses are trained in the morning, from dawn until 10 AM. After that the track has to be prepared for the races, which begin around noon. Every horse that needs to be trained—whether a gentle workout, breeze, gallop, or hard workout—needs a rider. Sometimes that rider is a jockey; sometimes it is an exercise rider, someone whose job it is to help train the horses but who does not ride in the races.

Calvin worked horses every morning, even if he was racing that day. He also studied videos of all the horses he was going to ride against to see whether they liked to run in front or come from behind and at what point in the race he should look out for them. This helped him know how to run his own horse, whether to follow the leaders or break early, for example.

Calvin did this to prepare for every race, no matter how big or small. And the Kentucky Oaks would be big. He would need every advantage he could get to win the prestigious race. Most everyone who comes to Churchill Downs for the Derby also watches the Oaks. Just like the racetrack has its famous twin spires, it also has its famous twin races. The crowds and the publicity would be huge.

Hal was cautiously optimistic. On the one hand, Rachel had been running well ever since Calvin got on her back, and Churchill Downs was her home track. On the other, this race would be the longest she had ever run. Brett was nervous. He thought Rachel had a really good chance at winning, but only if everything went smoothly in the days leading up to the big race. Both men prayed that Rachel wouldn't get overly tired or, worse, injure herself as race day approached.

Lead-up to the Kentucky Oaks

"JUST TAKE HER OUT for a gallop," Hal said to Calvin on the Monday morning before the Friday race.

"Yes, boss," Calvin answered. Calvin often worked the horses he was scheduled to race. He also cleaned stalls, walked horses, and bathed them for his brother, Cecil, who also was a trainer.

Rachel and Calvin headed onto the track. This six-furlong gallop would be her last workout before the race. As Rachel trotted toward the starting area, a blaring sound, like someone leaning on a car horn, shattered the early-morning peace. A horse had thrown its rider and gotten loose. A loose horse can cause collisions, injuries, and more. All the riders knew to gather their horses by the rail and stay there until the loose horse was caught. Calvin, in fact, took Rachel to the shedrow area, where she walked for 30 minutes, waiting for the track to clear. Calvin kept a sharp eye on Rachel. Many horses get nervous and "tie up," getting sometimes-debilitating cramps in their muscles when something out of the ordinary like this happens. But Rachel waited patiently, as steady as always. Soon the loose horse was caught, and Rachel began her workout.

Unfortunately, Rachel did not get the memo that this was supposed to be a relaxed gallop workout. She took off as if it were race day. She ran ⅝ of a mile in 58 seconds. That was a time that would have been good for a really fast horse in a race, let alone in practice. But that's not all! After they crossed the wire Calvin jiggled his foot a little to make it more comfortable in the webbing, he says—or maybe he knew they had an audience and he wanted to show what Rachel could do. Either way, she took off again, running full speed. She ran another furlong to finish her ¾-mile workout in a blistering 1:10 (one minute, ten seconds).

Hal and Brett were furious. Calvin tried to calm them down.

"Five days out?" Hal said to Calvin. "You're not supposed to do that."

"Mr. Hal," Calvin said, "I never asked her. She had her ears pricked. She came off the track bouncing and bouncing. She just went out there and had fun."

Rachel and Calvin training. *Suzie Oldham*

Calvin never had to ask; Rachel gave it her all.

Brett was so mad he stomped to the office and shut the door. He didn't come out again until he had calmed down. What if Rachel had been hurt? What if she wore herself out? Why was Calvin pushing her like that after they had agreed she would have an easy workout? Hal just shook his head and then kept a careful eye on Rachel that evening to make sure there was no heat in her legs.

But Rachel was not affected. With her usual vigor, she attacked the tetherball that was tied at the front of her stall for her to play with. Her ears were up. Her appetite was strong.

Hal, just to be safe, gave her an extra day of walking, "more to calm the trainer than restore the filly," one reporter wrote.

Her trainers may have had jitters, but Rachel, the reigning queen of the track, was unperturbed. Her fellow fillies provided no challenge; she won every race by five lengths and more. So the question many fans were asking was, where and how will she be challenged? Can she compete with and maybe even beat the boys? Her fans certainly thought so, and many insiders did too. On the track other trainers would ask Hal, "How's your big filly today?" Most important, she had that unusually long stride, and was very well proportioned. Zenyatta, another successful filly who was one year older than Rachel Alexandra, also was large. At 17 hands, Zenyatta was even larger than Rachel Alexandra, but it was Rachel's stride that set her apart.

Meanwhile, that week there was another Rachel at Churchill Downs, a young girl from the small town of Chillicothe, Illinois, who had been very sick with aplastic anemia, a bone marrow disease. Doctors tried everything to save her, and their last hope was a bone marrow transplant. For that operation, Rachel stayed in the hospital for four months straight. The transplant appeared to be successful, though even after she came home she had little energy or appetite, getting nutrition through an IV.

Rachel wanted to watch the Kentucky Derby, and the Make-a-Wish Foundation, which grants wishes to children who have life-threatening illnesses, made her wish come true. The foundation made a grand gesture: they didn't just bring Rachel to the Derby; they also brought her mom, dad, and brother Eric to Churchill Downs for the entire week. On Wednesday John Asher, head of publicity at the track, was giving Rachel and her family a tour around the **backside**, behind the scenes at a racetrack, including all the racehorse stabling, the track kitchen, dormitories for racetrack staff, recreation areas, and more. And he brought them by Rachel Alexandra's stall.

"Hal, here are some people I'd like you to meet," he said to Hal. And he introduced Rachel and her family. Hal picked up little Rachel, who was tiny for her age and wearing a face mask so she wouldn't catch germs, and helped her give big Rachel a pat on her nose. Rachel Alexandra politely acknowledged the little girl. Hal was smitten with the child.

Little Rachel was quiet and frail, but her eyes were like enormous sponges, soaking in the sights of the backside. Hal invited her to come to the saddling paddock on Friday, the day of the Oaks.

It was dark, and the early spring air had a chill to it when Hal left his house at 4:30 AM that Friday. He got to the barn just before 5 and, just like every day, checked on Rachel before going for coffee. And just like every day, Rachel heard Hal coming and poked her head out of her stall to greet him with a nuzzle, looking in his pockets for the peppermints she liked so much.

Horses have a reputation for liking carrots and apples, and plenty of them do. But a lot of horses also like peppermints. Hal fed Rachel peppermints every morning. Once he made sure she had eaten every bit of food from her bucket, Hal went to the backside kitchen for coffee and to start his day, wisecracking with the other trainers. You can tell a lot about a horse by how much it eats. If she doesn't finish her oats and grain, if some of it stays behind in her bucket, the trainers check the horse's temperature, check her legs for heat or inflammation, and generally sleuth around until they find an explanation for the loss of appetite. Rachel never left any food behind. She always cleaned her tub, her rubbery lips vacuuming up every oat and groat.

Since Rachel was racing today, she didn't go to the track in the morning. Rubin walked her around in the shedrow. Then she got a warm, sudsy bath. This was the biggest day of her racing career, and all the people around her were keyed up.

Normally people could come by anytime to take pictures and admire Rachel, but today was different. No one was allowed near her. Today the shedrow was barricaded with sawhorses, and security officers patrolled along the shedrow. Everyone—the grooms and riders, even the security officers—tried to be quiet around Rachel so she could feel calm.

Today was also different because Renée Wiggins had ordered dozens of pink baseball caps that said ALEXANDRA THE GREAT on them. Churchill Downs staff provided big pink RACHEL ALEXANDRA buttons too. Everyone who came by the barn got a cap, and soon Rachel Alexandra fans filled the stands with their pink ball caps and buttons.

Soon the race would begin. Hal quickly changed out of his jeans and cowboy boots and into a gray suit with a pink tie, topping off his outfit with an ALEXANDRA THE GREAT ball cap.

Hats are a big part of the Kentucky Derby and Kentucky Oaks regalia. Most women wear hats—the fancier the better. Renée's black hat with its big, wide brim contrasted dramatically with her silver hair and pink silk suit.

Rachel began her parade from the shedrow to the saddling paddock followed by more than a dozen people: Hal and Renée, their sons Lon and Whitney, Whitney's wife Alisa, several grandchildren, Hal's mom, their friend Jo Hooker, and numerous other friends and neighbors.

"Good luck!" "Go Rachel!" "Yay Rachel!" called the grooms, the exercise riders, and other members of the backside community, all waving from their perches on the fences along the shedrows.

It is close to half a mile from Rachel's number 16 stall to the saddling paddock. After they walked along the backside, the entourage stepped onto the track itself and walked, in full view of the grandstands and the cheering crowds, past the winner's circle to another break in the grandstand, where a tunnel leads to the saddling paddock.

This was the biggest crowd that Rachel had ever seen: 100,000 strong. They made a lot of noise. Hal tuned them out, concentrating on the steps of the race preparation as they walked in front of the cheering fans. Renée, on the other hand, tried to absorb everything. Seeing all the well-wishers and the bright colors, she got a lump in her throat. *It's like I'm having someone else's dream, someone else's life*, she thought. As the crowd yelled for her, Rachel looked around like a queen viewing her subjects, seemingly acknowledging their admiration with grace and dignity.

When they got to the saddling paddock, Rachel strolled into the stall. Rubin held her while Hal tacked her up. Hal put on her saddle pad and then the black saddlecloth sporting a bright yellow number 6, indicating her gate number. Next came Calvin's saddle. Dozens of people milled around in the paddock watching Rachel getting ready for her race, including little Rachel.

"If we win, I want you to be in the winners' circle with us too. Don't forget," Hal told the little girl, kneeling down to look her in the eyes. Rachel, her eyes wide, nodded. Then Hal and Renée gave little Rachel a gift bag full of Rachel Alexandra memorabilia, including a Rachel Alexandra baseball cap signed by Calvin, and some photographs. Each filly entered in the Kentucky

Oaks that year had received a one-of-a-kind pink leather halter with her name engraved on a brass nameplate. Hal included *that* in Rachel's gift bag too! Here was one of the biggest days of Hal's life, and he was determined to share it with a little girl from small-town Illinois.

Calvin walked across a balcony and then down the temporary staircase set up just for the Oaks and the Derby. The staircase ended just at the passage where the horses entered the saddling paddock. That way diminutive jockeys did not have to fight the shoulder-to-shoulder crowds that filled the plaza around the paddock.

Rachel and Calvin in the saddling paddock, led by Rubin.
Jo Hooker

He gave little Rachel a hug. Little Rachel gave her namesake a good luck pat. Calvin got on his dinner-plate-size saddle and grasped the reins. Other horses were high stepping, prancing about, and shaking their heads. Rachel was her regular serene self, walking like she was going out to pasture.

"Make sure you're at the winner's circle if we win," Hal told little Rachel again. Rachel nodded. Her father grinned. Together they watched Calvin and Rachel Alexandra parade around the paddock with the other fillies. Then the fillies headed to the starting gate.

The rest of the trainers knew they were mostly racing for second place.

"Maybe if they made her break from *behind* the gate," joked trainer Bob Baffert when asked how his horse might beat Rachel.

And They're Off!

AND THEY'RE OFF! are three of the most thrilling words in horse racing.

Rachel Alexandra had a good start, but Gabby's Golden Gal grabbed the early lead. Clods of dirt flew from the track as Rachel's hooves punched down like pistons. Calvin settled Rachel in behind Gabby. Then, at the second and final turn, with 3½ furlongs to go, Rachel crept up alongside her competitor and passed her as if Gabby were standing still. Jockey Victor Espinoza's arms pumped and pumped, urging his horse to keep up, but Gabby's Golden Gal was done, fading to sixth place.

Calvin sat, quiet as a shadow, not moving a muscle, while Rachel's enormous stride ate up the ground. With a quarter mile to go, she shifted into another gear and destroyed the field. She ran the last furlong in 12 seconds, without Calvin asking her to do a thing.

The announcer went crazy: "Rachel Alexandra is cruising in the lead! Calvin looks over his right shoulder, no danger! He looks over his left shoulder, no danger! She is romping home, absolutely cruising! Rachel Alexandra, winner of the Kentucky Oaks! It was a one horse race! That filly, Rachel Alexandra, brilliant!"

Before he even hit the finish line, Calvin looked into the stands and shook his finger four times, then pointed to Rachel as if to say, *Look at my girl. She is number one.* Then he was patting her neck and stroking her mane, and the race was won.

"I know she's a filly," said Calvin after the race, "but she's just like a colt. She's got the power. She's built like a house, and she does what you want her to do. And she loves it."

Rachel won the race by 20¼ lengths, the largest margin in history. And yet, she was not even pressed. On Monday, when she had cruised that extra six furlongs after her workout, her time was faster than her first six furlongs in the Oaks. She was just toying with her competition. That girl loved to run. And she ran smart, not all-out crazy all the time but putting on the speed when needed.

Trotting back to the winner's circle after the race, Rachel's stride was as perky as if she hadn't just smashed the Kentucky Oaks field.

Reed Palmer

Michael Andruso

Rachel left the competition in the dust at the Kentucky Oaks.

Hal's entourage, standing at the rail, didn't even see the finish. They were engulfed in group hysteria, hugging and yelling, jumping up and down, and crying for joy.

"I thought she had it when I took her to the paddock," Hal said later with a quiet smile on his weathered face and a tear on his cheek.

Hal, Dolph, and their families and friends traipsed to the winner's circle. Little Rachel and her dad met them there. Calvin was still on Rachel Alexandra's back,

Rachel winning the Kentucky Oaks, with the Churchill Downs spires in the background. *Barbara Livingston*

overcome with emotion and holding the blanket of lilies draped over her **withers**. The Derby is known as the Run for the Roses, and the winner gets a blanket of red roses. The Oaks winner gets lilies, as in lilies for the fillies.

The winner's circle was mobbed. TV sports announcer Bob Costas was there. Then, after Calvin dismounted, Hal picked up little Rachel, in her sweet spring dress and her face mask, so she was right in the thick of things. In the midst of accepting the trophy, Hal kept checking

Trophy presentation, from left: Little Rachel, Hal Wiggins, Renée Wiggins, Ellen Morrison, and Calvin Borel. *Reed Palmer*

with Rachel's dad, making the *OK* signal with a question on his face: *Is this OK for Rachel?* he wanted to know.

Then Hal and Renée and even little Rachel went to a press conference. There they got to watch the replay of the whole race. For the first time they appreciated just how much Rachel had won by. Meanwhile, Rachel Alexandra went to her regular stall, carrying her blanket of lilies on her shoulders. Rachel Alexandra was cooled down and bathed. She walked into her stall, stall 17 in barn 30. Her blanket of lilies was draped from the low cinderblock wall in front of her door. She ate her customary oats and grain in her stall, just like every other day.

"She's so big and yet she's so light on herself," remarked Calvin later that day. "That's what makes her a good horse. If you watch, other horses take three strides to her one. When you're on her you can feel it. [It feels like] she's just loafing, and it's like, 'Somebody's got to be coming.' She's unbelievable."

When they got home that night, Hal and Renée sat together on the couch answering congratulatory texts and e-mails. Hal said it was a day like any other day, but the dress shoes he wore that day—the ones he wore when he paraded with Rachel Alexandra around the track before the race, the ones he wore accepting the trophy for the Kentucky Oaks after the race—are carefully preserved in a plastic bag in his closet. They still have that day's Churchill Downs racetrack sand on them.

Calvin was overcome with emotion after winning the Kentucky Oaks with Rachel. *Reed Palmer*

Kentucky Derby Surprise

THE DAY AFTER THE Oaks—Kentucky Derby Day—
Hal went to check on Rachel. She was walking around
the barn with her groom, Rubin, as usual, but with so
much energy, she practically dragged him. After such
a strong race, trainers expect their horse to have lower
energy the next day or two, but Rachel's epic performance had apparently taken almost nothing out of her.

Most of Rachel's lilies were gone, given away. But the
crowds of well-wishers kept coming. Hal did not have
a horse in the Derby, but he and Renée joined the fes-
tivities, watching the race on a TV in the shedrow and
hosting their annual potluck, complete with Memphis
barbecue, down by the stalls.

Meanwhile, Calvin had work to do. He was riding Mine That Bird, a horse that had 50-to-1 odds and was unknown on the American horse racing circuit but had run well in Canada. Calvin had studied the films and seen that Mine That Bird liked to run in the back. He liked to come from behind to win. That is a hard place for jockeys to run. They have to fight the urge to put their horse in the race too early. In the films Calvin saw that happen with Mine That Bird, taking the lead too early and then getting caught the last 50 yards. Calvin knew he had to sit back, wait, and be patient. That takes nerves as tough as the calluses on a jockey's hands.

The day of the Derby was cool and sunny, but things were looking stormy for Calvin and Mine That Bird as their race began. It's one thing to run in the back of the pack, but Mine That Bird trailed so far behind the 20-horse field that the TV cameras didn't show him. Then Calvin stomped on the accelerator, and Mine That Bird took off, working his way up through the herd. Mine That Bird was in 19th place, then 18th, and then he barreled into 10th.

Maybe I can get a check, Calvin thought.

Mine That Bird might finish first, second, or third and earn some prize money, or "finish in the money." If that happened, it meant Calvin would get paid more than the roughly $50 jockeys get for riding a race. Then, around the last turn, Calvin tightened up the reins, an action that signaled to the horse that if he had more energy, now was the time to give it. Mine That Bird flew forward, fresh and strong. Calvin couldn't believe it! He knew in that moment he would win the race. He had earned the nickname Calvin Bo-rail because he liked to ride so close to the rail the white paint comes off on his boot. Sure enough, Mine That Bird came up along the rail, threading between horses, stunning the fans by winning—and not just by a head; he won by 6¾ lengths.

That was the second-biggest upset in Derby history, behind Donerail who won at 91-to-1 odds. It was also the greatest winning margin since Assault won by eight lengths in 1946. The crowd went wild. Everyone in Rachel's shedrow was screaming and yelling in excitement.

In two days Calvin had won both the Oaks and the Derby. He became only the seventh jockey in history to win both races in the same year. Not bad for a poor Cajun boy who grew up on his family's sugarcane farm dreaming of riding in the Derby. Calvin had ridden in the Derby 11 times now, winning it 3 times and coming in third twice. He was six rides away from 5,000 career wins.

Meanwhile, Hal was planning for Rachel's next race. The one-mile Acorn Stakes at Belmont Park on June 6 would give her the right amount of rest time between races. In 2009 the Acorn was part of the **Triple Tiara** (the filly equivalent of the Triple Crown). The races that complete the Triple Tiara vary from year to year, but this year the other two races were the Mother Goose and the Coaching Club American Oaks. Coincidentally, the Acorn would take place the same day as the Belmont Stakes, the third race in the Triple Crown and a race that many Rachel fans thought she should enter instead. That way she could race against the boys.

But then something happened to completely derail Hal's careful plans.

10

Rachel Is Sold

HAL AND RENÉE WERE still getting congratulatory notes and calls three days after the Derby, when they had a conversation with Dolph that trampled their hearts.

"I sold Rachel Alexandra," he told them over the phone. "She's leaving your barn and going to Jess Jackson's barn."

Jess Jackson, the founder and owner of Kendall-Jackson winery and a horse enthusiast, was able to pour enormous amounts of money into his hobby. He had a very large racing operation, based at Stonestreet Farms in Lexington, that included dozens of outstanding horses, including the 2007 Horse of the Year, Curlin.

After the Kentucky Oaks, Jess had called Dolph. "I want to buy your filly and breed her to Curlin," he said.

"Well, Jess, she's not for sale. I don't want to sell her," Dolph answered.

"If you *were* gonna sell her, what would you want for her?"

"I wouldn't take a penny less than $10 million," Dolph said, thinking no one would be crazy enough to pay that kind of money for a filly, no matter how good she was.

But Jess said, "I'll take her!"

"You're kidding me. You'd pay $10 million for a horse?" Dolph was flabbergasted.

"For that one I would," Jess answered.

Paying that kind of money for a filly was unheard of, though an outstanding stallion will sell for that much and more.

"My lawyer and your lawyer will meet in Louisville," Dolph told him. "You have a cashier's check. I don't sell a horse except for a cashier's check even though I know you, no matter how much money you got."

Hal couldn't believe his fairy tale had ended almost as soon it began. To feel that kind of ecstasy and jubilation and then, before he had time to get used to those top-of-the-world feelings, to learn that the best horse he'd ever trained was no longer his to train? That was hard. Hal tried not to become too attached to any one horse, but that was difficult to do with Rachel. She was so calm and smart, it was impossible not to feel connected to her. Hal and Renée walked around numb for days.

It was not their decision, of course. Dolph called the shots. He had become attached to Rachel Alexandra too.

He never would have sold her, he said, but Jess offered "crazy money" for her. As a businessman, it was unthinkable to turn the offer down.

Jess and Dolph met at Dolph's bank in Lexington just four short days after Rachel Alexandra had won the Oaks, and Jess handed over a cashier's check. The deal was done.

Maybe in a Hollywood movie Rachel would have stayed in Hal's barn, but this was real life. As much as he tried to minimize his disappointment and continue training, it was a blow to lose her.

At 5:15 AM on Thursday, May 7, Rachel walked the 200 yards that separated her old barn from her new one. Trainers Steve Asmussen and Scott Blasi, Brett's friend, would train Rachel for Jess.

Rachel was gone, moved just a few shedrows over. Hal and his staff were heartsick. Everyone walked around with their heads down in mourning. But Hal let his workers grieve for only a moment. He called them together and told everyone, "Hey, we had a lot of fun with her. Sun's gonna keep coming up." Then he put another horse in Rachel's stall so that his staff didn't have to look at an empty spot.

Hal retired not long afterward and moved with Renée to Houston, where their grandchildren lived. He missed those days on the backside of Churchill Downs but continued to serve as a consultant in the horse industry.

Rachel settled into her new barn, with her new trainers and new routines, just as she did everything; with barely a twitch of her tail, she took these changes in stride.

Calvin's Decision

RUMORS HAD BEEN swirling ever since the Kentucky Oaks that Rachel was being sold; the whole racetrack community knew the veterinarian had examined her. Calvin was worried. If Rachel was sold, what if the new owners didn't want him to ride her? For several days the jockey felt tense and unsettled. He didn't want anything to change. But he knew he had to be patient and pick his moment, just like he was so good at doing on the track. He didn't want to approach the new owners before the sale happened.

Then he heard the news that it was official: Rachel had indeed been sold to Jess Jackson and his wife, Barbara Banke, owners of Stonestreet Farms. The morning the sale was announced, Calvin called Lisa from the "jock's room"—the jockeys' locker room and lounge—to tell her the news.

Here he was coming off one of the biggest highs of his career, he said, winning both the Derby and the Oaks in a single weekend. He had in his hand a check for $141,720, his share of the Kentucky Derby prize. But he was upset because he didn't know if he would ever sit on his beloved Rachel again.

How could so much sadness and so much joy fit inside one heart at the same time? The Derby check represented more than just money to Calvin; it meant he had achieved his dream of being an outstanding professional jockey. But he would tear it up in a skinny minute if it meant he could keep riding Rachel. Chances were good, he lamented to Lisa, that Jess would have his regular rider, jockey Robby Albarado, ride his newest filly.

Lisa suggested that Calvin speak with the new owners as soon as he could. "To be on the safe side," she said. She knew Calvin could make a good case for why he should ride Rachel. Rachel and Calvin had a rapport, a special connection. Surely the owners would understand and appreciate that?

Calvin decided to take Lisa's advice. It never hurt to ask, he knew. He drove home that day in a daze, so worried about what the next day would bring.

At 4:30 the next morning, in the cool, calm darkness, Calvin hitched up his britches and went to Rachel's barn to talk to her new owners. The sound of contented horses munching oats filled the air. Calvin was nervous. He found Jess, Barbara, and trainer Steve Asmussen at the barn.

"Mr. Jackson, I'd love to ride the filly," Calvin said to Jess. He was prepared to beg, but he didn't have to.

"She's your horse," Jess answered. "I plan to run her in the Preakness."

In one moment Calvin's heart swooped up high, like a bird in the sky; Rachel and he could keep riding together! And in the next it was as if a hawk had grabbed his heart in its talons. Calvin had already agreed to ride Mine That Bird in the Preakness, less than two weeks away.

As winner of the Derby on Mine That Bird, Calvin was the only jockey in the world who had a chance this year to make a play for the Triple Crown—a rare event. It had been more than 30 years since a horse had won the Crown. The last was in 1978, when Affirmed, ridden by jockey Steve Cauthen, fought off challenges by Alydar to grab the plum of Thoroughbred racing. If Calvin stuck with Mine That Bird, he knew he had the next shot at the Crown.

Calvin's face, always expressive, showed everything: his joy and his concern. He would have to give up Mine That Bird in order to ride Rachel. Still, it wasn't a very hard decision. He had always made clear to Mine That Bird's handlers that if he ever had to choose mounts, there was no contest; he would ride Rachel every time. Rachel Alexandra was the best horse of the thousands

he had ridden in his life. He felt an emotional connection to her that was more important to him than money,
prestige, or even a prominent place in racing history. He
went with his gut, just like he did on the track. He chose
his love—and the better horse—Rachel Alexandra, giving up any hope for a Triple Crown.

"Rachel means more to Calvin than the Triple
Crown," Lisa said. (In fact, Mine That Bird did not go
on to win the Triple Crown. That feat wasn't accomplished again until 2015, by the Thoroughbred American Pharoah.)

Rachel, meanwhile, had no worries. She now lived
in Curlin's old stall and seemed right at home. She had
changed barns, changed trainers, changed exercise riders, and changed her feed, but she did not bat an eye. She
enjoyed her new menu, which included cooked oats, and
never missed a meal.

As soon as his meeting was over, a greatly relieved
Calvin called Lisa to tell her the good news. Then he
went straight to Mine That Bird's barn, to tell his owners, Mark Allen and Chip Wooley, that they would have
to find another mount for their horse.

No jockey in history had come off a Derby winner
to ride another horse in a Triple Crown race. One time,
however, back in 1975, the undefeated filly Ruffian and
Derby winner Foolish Pleasure shared the same jockey,
Jacinto Vasquez. When their match race was scheduled,
Jacinto had to choose between them. He too chose the
filly; he chose Ruffian.

Calvin considered what it meant for Rachel to race against the boys. No one really knew yet what she could do. She hadn't been asked to run her hardest. Added to that, the last time a filly had won the Preakness, Calvin Coolidge was president, radio was in its infancy, transcontinental airmail service had just begun, the Great Depression had not yet occurred, and women had only just been given the right to vote. Maybe the Preakness wasn't a race for fillies.

The media and the fans went to town talking about what Calvin should do. Challenges abounded, they said: Rachel had never raced a full 9½ furlongs, the length of the Preakness; with 13 horses in the field, it would be the most horses she had ever raced against at one time; and it would also be Rachel's first trip to the East Coast.

The next morning, as Calvin stood at Rachel's stall door caressing her nose and feeding her carrots, he pondered the obstacles. True, he didn't know for sure that Rachel could run hard for 9½ furlongs. He didn't know for sure that she could compete against colts and beat them, but then again, nothing is ever certain in racing.

What Calvin did know for sure was that Rachel was a true athlete and would give it her best. A new track and large crowds would not bother her, Calvin knew. And he knew that Rachel was the faster horse, as surely as he knew horses had hooves. No horse could outrun her, not with him on her back.

But horse racing is always a gamble. Which is to say, what if she got blocked or had a bad start? It could happen. What if she lost? Would Jess put a different jockey on her? Would Jess take his beloved Rachel away from Calvin? *If we lose, could I lose her?* Calvin worried.

But Jess and Barbara calmed his fears. "Listen, Calvin," they said, "we're doing the impossible. Don't worry about that. She is yours. If you get beat, you get beat." Jess and Barbara were so confident in Calvin that the jockey relaxed a little. He felt blessed, but apprehension lingered. This was too much good luck for one man. He would have to be made of stone to not worry about his decision. And Calvin, the jockey who wore his heart on his sleeve, was not made of stone. He did, however, have nerves of steel.

The Preakness

TWELVE HORSES WERE scheduled to run the Preakness, but there was space for 14. So now that Calvin was on board, all Jess Jackson had to do was whip out his checkbook and pay a $100,000 supplemental entry fee for not having nominated Rachel to the race earlier in the season. The filly had not been nominated for any of the Triple Crown races, since at that deadline Dolph owned her and steadfastly refused to race her against colts.

One hundred thousand dollars was no hardship for the multimillionaire; he was on a mission to see what heights Rachel could soar to. But before Jess could execute his plan, several owners tried to fill the empty slots with their own, slower horses.

At the beginning of the racing season, owners pay a fee to nominate their horses for any race they might want to run in the upcoming racing season. A horse that has been nominated is not required to race, so often owners nominate their horses for more races than they ever would run, just to save a place and give themselves options. This nomination gives a horse preference over a horse that wasn't nominated but wants to run the race.

Mark Allen, one of Mine That Bird's owners, wanted to add Indy Express, a horse that had never won a race, to the field in order to prevent Rachel Alexandra from running. Pioneerof the Nile's owner, Ahmed Zayat, had nominated 20 horses, so he also intended to add another of his ponies to the race.

It was like a boys' treehouse with a big sign on it: No GIRLS ALLOWED. In this case the boys were scared: they knew this girl had a good chance of beating the pants off them.

Finally, someone—a woman—put a stop to their shenanigans.

"We are for sportsmanship and what's best for the game," announced Marylou Whitney, co-owner of Luv Gov, one of the horses already entered in the Preakness. "If we are the deciding factor on whether or not Rachel Alexandra gets in, then we'll withdraw and wait for the Belmont."

With that declaration, Marylou assured that Rachel would have a spot and made the other trainers and owners realize they were being pitifully poor sports. Jess had a dozen roses sent to Marylou in thanks for her gesture in support of Rachel Alexandra.

Mark Allen came around quickly. "She might kick our butts," he said of Rachel Alexandra, "but she deserves a shot."

In the week leading up to the race, stories about Rachel and her chances dominated the sports pages. Reporters dutifully noted that no filly had won the Preakness since their own grandparents were children. They expressed concern about the condition of the track, with heavy rain forecast. They acknowledged the other strong competitors in the field: Rachel would race against Mine That Bird, the winner of the Derby; Pioneer of the Nile, the Derby runner-up and winner of three other big races; and Big Drama, who had not been beaten in his last six races.

But still, every owner and trainer the sportswriters interviewed said Rachel was exceptional, sensational, Secretariat-like, one for the ages. The betting public agreed: Rachel was the clear favorite heading into the race.

The day of the race, 77,000 people poured into Pimlico racetrack in Baltimore, Maryland. Families—mothers and daughters, fathers and sons—swarmed the infield. The band ZZ Top played live on the bandstand. While children played beach volleyball, parents placed bets, bought food, and watched the racing on two jumbo screens.

In the jocks' room, Calvin put on the silks—the jockey's uniform—for Jess's team: bright, cocky, eye-stopping yellow with a maroon *V*. Silks, which used to be made of silk but now are Lycra and polyester, help identify the horses during the race. Owners create their own unique designs, and every design is registered.

Calvin weighed in: 110 pounds of sinewy muscle. His nephew, Shane Borel, who worked as his valet—the person who keeps track of the jockey's equipment—carried his tack (goggles, saddle, pad, stirrups) to the saddling paddock. It had begun to drizzle.

Assigning starting gates is a random, luck-of-the-draw process, and Rachel had been unlucky. She would start from the 13th position, or post, the farthest from the rail. No horse had ever won from that gate.

Did Calvin feel the pressure? Sure he did. But he had spent his life racing. He knew with the calm assurance of a world-class athlete that he would ride his best, and Rachel would give her best. That was all they could do.

Calvin took a deep breath and strode to the saddling paddock. He knew if he lost, he could look stupid, but, thanks to Jess's confidence in him, he felt relaxed and calm. Besides, there were worse things in life than looking stupid, like not taking a chance on a once-in-a-lifetime horse, like not giving a once-in-a-lifetime horse her chance to make racing history.

How about Rachel? Did she feel the pressure, the tension in the air? Scott had schooled her in the saddling paddock a couple times during the week, and she'd had a couple of gallops on the track, so she knew what was coming.

She's a racehorse, and she likes her job, Scott thought.

In the saddling paddock, Rachel posed. She held her head up high, her ears forward and her eyes bright. She was revved and ready to run. But she was a professional and stood patiently while her groom adjusted Calvin's minuscule racing saddle on her back.

"Go get it done," trainer Steve Asmussen said to Calvin.

Calvin gave a quick nod, and Steve gave him a leg up on Rachel's glorious back.

"Let's go, big mama. Let's go, sweetie," he said as they headed for the gates.

The crowd yelled for Calvin. He waved back. They cheered for Rachel. She kept her eyes forward and her gait stately. Her body, which had grown and strengthened over the past year, was magnificent. She was focused and ready to run.

A Dazzling Display

THIRTEEN JOCKEYS mounted 13 horses, and 13 grooms led each one to the starting gate. Take the Points argued with his jockey by tossing his head and prancing. Big Drama reared in the gate, throwing his jockey and almost flipping over. Rachel strolled to the gate as she had so many times before, head down, body relaxed. Today her mane was braided instead of flowing free, and her jockey wore different colors, but nothing else had changed. She was there to run and to win, like always.

Rachel took her three deep breaths and stepped into the gate. The bell jangled, and the gates banged opened, releasing a thunder of hooves and flying tails. With each hoof pounding on the track a puff of dust flew—puff, puff, puff, like a steam engine.

Rachel Alexandra had stumbled breaking from the far gate, but she still managed to shoulder her way to the front of the 13-horse field, her white, upside-down exclamation-point blaze shining like a beacon. *No horse has ever won the race from that gate? We'll see about that,* Rachel Alexandra seemed to say.

Hooves flying the fastest, stride the longest, tail streaming, ears up, relaxed and fast, Rachel Alexandra ran in front of 12 three-year-old colts, her beloved jockey perched on her back and urging her on. Six long strides into the race, Calvin pulled down his first pair of goggles.

Even though she had stumbled, even though she had a hard time running in the deep, soft track, and even though she was fighting off a challenge from Big Drama, Rachel kept her stride easy.

After ¼ mile, Calvin pulled off his second pair of goggles. Rachel ran the first ½ mile at 46 seconds, faster than her Kentucky Oaks run by more than a second. With ⅜ of a mile to go, Rachel shifted into another gear and split from the field, opening up six lengths of daylight between her and the second-place horse.

With less than a furlong (about the length of two football fields) to go, Mine That Bird, the horse that loved to run from behind, made his famous move. Mine That Bird's hooves pounded, his neck stretched with each stride. And, just like at the Derby, he picked off horses one by one.

Soon only Rachel, smooth and quick, flew ahead of him. Calvin knew Mine That Bird was coming. Rachel did too; the vibrations of Mine That Bird's pounding hooves spurred her on. Rachel extended her stride, but her feet slipped in the deep, loose track.

"C'mon!" yelled Calvin, raising his whip to her for the first time ever.

Rachel had led the whole long, fast race, and now Calvin was asking her for more. Could she give it? Did she have more in her tank?

Rachel stretched out her neck, dug deep, and held on, repulsing Mine That Bird's challenge.

Mine That Bird gave it his all, but he could not catch Alexandra the Great.

The crowd went bonkers. Arms waving, hats waving, they roared and stomped and jumped in ecstasy.

"Mine That Bird tried to close the gap but Rachel is simply above and beyond him," yelled the announcer, his voice raw. "We've seen history! A dazzling display by Rachel Alexandra, the first filly to win the Preakness in 85 years!"

After Rachel and Calvin crossed the finish line, Calvin stood up in his stirrups and dropped his head; all the worry and stress of the previous weeks evaporated, and he suddenly felt exhausted and emotionally overwhelmed. He had become the first jockey in history ever to win the first two legs of the Triple Crown on different horses.

"How good she really might be we don't know yet," said Jess later. "She wants to win. She's got an attitude. You see it in the great horses. It's the eye of the eagle."

Rachel galloped gently for several more furlongs. When the track pony came to get her, Rachel's ears stood up high. She looked around happily, as if she could run the race again. She walked back toward the winner's circle while the fans yelled and cheered. Calvin waved to them, a grin radiating from his face.

He took a sponge full of water and squeezed it over Rachel's head, drenching her. Scott took the filly's **shank**, her muzzle drooling onto his brown suit and tie. Calvin leaned down and wrapped his hand around Scott's neck, pulling him close. Scott's grin reflected Calvin's, the two men's faces showing their immense pride and joy.

As soon as Rachel had been officially declared the Preakness winner, a painter climbed up and gave the horse-and-jockey weathervane on the top of the cupola a new coat of paint. It is a Preakness tradition to paint the weathervane in the winning horse's colors, so Jess's bright-yellow silks with the maroon *V* would decorate the weathervane for the next 365 days.

"We know she can run against colts," Jess said after the race. "She is capable of doing this. She has the strength and endurance to make it work," he also said.

"The filly has engaged the sense of horseplayers and casual fans alike," wrote one sportswriter.

Everyone celebrated Rachel. Even people who didn't follow horse racing saw her in the magazines and newspapers they picked up. Famed *Vogue* magazine editor Anna Wintour had attended the Preakness and was so inspired by the filly that her magazine ran a photo spread of Rachel in all her glory. Rachel stood in her best horse shoes, Silver Queen size 6, looking over her shoulder, her magnificent neck arched, her dark-chocolate coat gleaming.

Vogue, a magazine that usually documents the latest in fine fashion and glamour, was instead celebrating this phenomenal filly who had shown the boys her heels. In the photos she appears slightly annoyed by the attention, while accepting it as her due.

She had shown the world that she could compete against colts and win, even with the disadvantage of having the farthest outside gate. It left fans wondering, what would she do next?

Rachel Fever

RACHEL ALEXANDRA had brought her game—not even her best game—to the boys and beat them at their own track. What was left to prove? Jess Jackson trotted Rachel up to the Mother Goose, a race at Belmont Park in Elmont, New York, that, along with the Acorn and the American Oaks Stakes, made up the Triple Tiara.

Only Malibu Prayer and Flashing showed up to race Rachel for the $270,000 purse at the Mother Goose. The Belmont track, thrilled with Rachel's presence, let all women in for free and gave away 10,000 pink rubber Rachel Alexandra bracelets to the 13,352 fans in attendance.

Racing fans who came to watch Rachel on this sunny, mild day might have expected the Mother Goose to be a glorified workout, but the other competitors had a different plan. Because Rachel Alexandra had just won the Preakness and become a star, the other jockeys really wanted to beat her. Malibu Prayer took off like a demon, with Flashing right behind her. Malibu Prayer's first half mile was a blistering 44 seconds, two seconds faster than Rachel's half mile at the Preakness.

For the first time in six starts, Rachel was not running in front or just off the front. But that did not worry Calvin. Some jockeys would panic or get impatient. Not Calvin. Rachel was running relaxed and laid back, but Calvin knew what she could do. Rachel just tucked herself in behind the leaders until the far turn, when Calvin gave her a little more rein, and she thrust right between the two front runners and into the lead. Then he cut her loose, and she won by almost 20 lengths, with a time of 1:46.33, breaking the track record and beating her own Kentucky Oaks time by two seconds. Ruffian, who is considered by many to be the best filly that ever ran, won the 1975 Triple Tiara, and Rachel demolished Ruffian's winning margin record of 13½ lengths. At the final pole, which indicated there was one more furlong, or 220 yards, left, Calvin was easing her. So Rachel did all that without even pushing herself.

She was less than one second off the **overall track record**, set by Secretariat in 1973.

Racing fans had been comparing her to Ruffian after the Preakness, but after the Mother Goose, Rachel Alexandra looked like the superior horse. For one thing,

Ruffian was always a little wild, always on the verge of hurting herself because she ran so hard, almost desperately. Twice she ran injured. Once she had a popped **splint**, which isn't a serious injury but is painful. That race she broke the stakes record. The last race of her two-year-old career, Ruffian also set a track record, but the next day her trainers discovered that she had a hairline fracture of her right hind leg. The horse had either not felt or run through the pain.

Rachel Alexandra was big and strong, just like Ruffian, but less reckless. Up until the Woodward, Rachel had won by a combined 63¾ lengths over nine races, which is almost 8 lengths on average, same as Ruffian. But the difference is, when Rachel raced the boys, she suffered no injuries as a result.

"She is a special filly," said Jess after the race. "She is a champion. She is a lady. We don't know where her bottom is. She just broke a track record, and she wasn't even asked."

Her trainer, Steve Asmussen, said, "She's a great athlete. She's just extremely endearing. She has a soft and kind look and feel. When she walks over, she takes those great big strides. Everything about her, she just excites you."

A month later, on August 2, Jess decided to race Rachel against the boys again, this time at the $1.25 million Haskell Invitational at Monmouth Park in New Jersey. The competition would be fierce: Summer Bird had won the Belmont Stakes, the third leg of the Triple Crown;

Papa Clem, the Arkansas Derby winner, also would be there among the older, stronger horses; and Munnings had just won two stakes victories. *Thoroughbred Daily News* wrote, "Munnings looms as the biggest threat to Rachel. The chestnut colt has earned triple digit Beyers in each of his three starts this season."

Rachel Alexandra rode in her van down to Monmouth from Saratoga two days before the race. That afternoon Scott schooled her in the paddock. Even though it was rainy, hot, and humid, Rachel's fans were there in force, clapping and calling out her name. More than 37,000 people gathered to see if the diva could once again beat the boys. Fans, most of them young girls, stood outside the winner's circle waving signs saying GIRL POWER; ROBUST RACHEL ALEXANDRA; YEAH, I RUN LIKE A GIRL, TRY TO KEEP UP!; and RACHEL ALEXANDRA THE GREAT, CONQUEROR OF THE BOYS. One girl wore a tiara adorned with the words CELEBRITY QUEEN. The gift shop was selling T-shirts with RUNS LIKE A GIRL emblazoned on the front. They sold out by 12:30.

Could she beat the boys again? Would the wet, sloppy track bother her? Or the heat and humidity?

At the gate, she went off like a cannon as the doors slammed open. Early in the seven-horse race, Munnings and Summer Bird were in the lead, with Rachel in third, just like at the Mother Goose.

Calvin and Rachel were happy to bide their time. Rachel would chase down the leaders. By the final turn,

Calvin greeting Rachel's fans after the race. *Bill Denver*

she had made her move, gaining the lead over Munnings and Summer Bird. Then, once again, Rachel shifted into that extra gear that was all her own. She quickly separated from her two rivals, hurtling down the straightaway, relaxed and smooth.

Rachel Alexandra won by six lengths, the second-greatest margin in the history of that race. Her winning time was 1:47.21, one-fifth of a second off the stakes

Rachel won the Haskell decisively. *Bill Denver*

record, set by Majestic Light in 1976, and two-fifths off the track record, set by Spend a Buck, who had won his race by a nose. Rachel Alexandra became only the second filly ever to win the Haskell. (Serena's Song won in 1995.) That day she earned a Beyer speed figure of 116, the highest of any horse in North America that year.

"The Haskell changed everything," wrote ESPN's Bill Finley. "After what she did last Sunday at Monmouth, demolishing a terrific collection of three-year old males, Rachel Alexandra is no longer just a very good filly or even a great filly. She has stepped into another realm. She is one of the very best fillies in the history of the sport, perhaps the best ever."

Will She Win
the Woodward?

JESS JACKSON NEXT entered Rachel Alexandra in the Woodward Stakes, one of the top races for horses of any age run at Saratoga Springs, New York, a month after the Haskell. Only the second filly to enter the race in 55 runnings, Rachel would compete against seven male horses in their prime. These horses, which ranged in age from four to six, were even bigger and stronger than the three-year-olds she had dominated at the Preakness and the Haskell.

The field would include five horses—Cool Coal Man, Bullsbay, It's a Bird, Macho Again, and Past the Point—who had all recently won races with Beyer numbers well above 100. Asiatic Boy, the first horse to win the

United Arab Emirates Triple Crown, also was entered. There were horses that would start out fast and some that would finish fast, so there was going to be no rest for Rachel Alexandra.

But Rachel was looking strong too. She seemed to be getting better with each race. The day after the Haskell, noted her training rider, Dominic Terry, "she was stronger than the day before the race." He added, "I'm waiting for the day that one of the races does tone her down a notch. When she came back after the Haskell I'm like, 'I know that had to affect her in some way,' and it just didn't."

The other trainers had noticed that as well.

"If they're talking about Ruffian and her in the same breath, there's nothing left to say," said Nicholas Zito, Cool Coal Man's trainer.

In the weeks leading up to the race, banners emblazoned with RACHEL ALEXANDRA: RUN LIKE A GIRL waved in the breeze up and down Broadway, Saratoga's main street. Photos and drawings of Rachel, sporting her trademark blaze, were everywhere: from a chimney sweep's van to the construction site for a new city center. In a three-foot-tall photo in the window of Saratoga Saddlery, Rachel was working out, larger than life, her nostrils flaring, her mane streaming.

In preparation for the race, Scott saddled Rachel and led her into the paddock just as if it were race day. Every day her fans gathered. They called her name, gave her an ovation, craned their necks, and snapped

Banners waved all over Saratoga Springs for Rachel Alexandra. *Barbara Livingston*

picture after picture. "She is being widely hailed as the most brilliant Thoroughbred of her sex since Ruffian, and her achievements dwarf those of the legendary filly who died tragically in 1975," wrote Andrew Beyer in the *Washington Post*.

The day of the Woodward the pure white moon glimmered in the dawn, the sky crimson as the sun rose. A light fog shrouded the racetrack. Even before 7 AM, crowds of people mashed the gates, wanting to stake a claim in the grounds. A record-breaking 31,171 fans came to Saratoga to witness history. Curlin, the previous year's Horse of the Year, had drawn only 23,000.

Fans sported big pink RACHEL buttons. Grown-ups wore them on their lapels. Little girls wore them on their T-shirts, one of which said FILLIES RULE, SARATOGA 2009. When fans flipped through their programs, the booklets flopped open to a center spread, a souvenir poster of Rachel that Jess paid for.

Scott and Rachel walked from the stable to the paddock. Crowds 10 people deep lined the path. Fathers held their daughters on their shoulders, straining to catch a glimpse of their hero.

In the jock's room, Calvin changed into Jess's silks and stepped on the scales, holding his saddle. Then he headed across the walkway to the saddling paddock. Hundreds of people lined his path.

In the saddling paddock, Rachel was wound up, the veins in her neck swelling, her white eye shining. Steve gave Calvin a leg up. Rachel and Calvin made two circuits around the paddock. Calvin brought up the rear of the jockeys.

Rachel was a mere nine furlongs away from cementing her place as the filly of the ages. And they would be the toughest nine furlongs she'd ever run.

Before she even got to the starting gate, Rachel suddenly became startled and reared up, her hooves pawing the sky. Calvin, startled himself, slid right off, loosening the reins as she reared.

"It's OK, big mama. It's OK," he said to her. Her hooves came back to the track. She and Calvin looked at one another. He climbed back on.

Some people think when a horse misbehaves, bucking and shying, it is telling its rider that it does not want to run. Perhaps Rachel was uncharacteristically wound up from all the tension in the air around her. Calvin thought perhaps the noise of the crowd, or a photographer standing on the turf where she had never seen a person before, may have spooked her.

Calvin knew he had to focus all his energy on Rachel, keeping her calm and collected, and getting her into the gate smoothly. After that, he knew, she'd be all in.

The real challenge was racing with a target on her back: every horse and jockey in the field would take a run at Rachel. Calvin knew the pace would be fast from the start of the race, but it would be a balancing act because Da' Tara and Cool Coal Man could catch Rachel if she used all her speed in the front half of the race. It would be up to Calvin to keep her on pace and from burning out early. There was also an added challenge: the Saratoga track was deep and sandy, making it hard for Rachel to get a grip on the track. It would be like trying to run on a beach. Saratoga is a track that wears out a lot of great horses.

After her scorchingly fast opening quarter (two furlongs) of 22.48 seconds, track announcer Tom Durkin bellowed, "There'll be no free ride for Rachel Alexandra. They're making her work for every step today."

Each horse took a turn challenging Rachel. First was 2008 Belmont Stakes winner Da' Tara. Then his stablemate Cool Coal Man, coming off an almost 13-length romp in the Albert the Great Stakes, charged her. Then, when those horses dropped back to recover after running the half mile in 46.24 seconds, Past the Point picked up the challenge, chasing Rachel, who ran the first three-quarters of a mile in a very fast 1:10.24. Rachel thwarted his bid as well.

Then came the big final assault. Bullsbay, who was so explosive in the Whitney, pulled up to Rachel's flank turning for home. Asiatic Boy and Macho Again also moved in, expecting to encounter a softened-up Rachel in the final furlong.

Calvin hit Rachel with his crop five times right-handed and then three times left-handed. Rachel turned back Bullsbay's challenge, but here came a fresh Macho Again, who had found a gaping hole at the top of the stretch and gave a valiant final effort, gaining momentum, turning on his famous late-race power surge. The charging gray stormed up alongside Rachel. The sound from the stands was deafening, fans yelling and screaming for Rachel.

Unlike Ruffian, Rachel did not need to always lead, but she never let a horse come up from behind. She would barely hear a horse and would rebreak, taking off like a hare. Macho's gray hide and pit-bull snout drew even with Rachel's right hip. Calvin hit her again. She had won every other race with her ears pricked, rarely feeling the sting of the whip. Calvin knew Rachel did not like getting hit, and he only rarely did so. But he also knew that this was the time; if she had anything left, Rachel had to give it now. His arm flogging, Calvin barraged his filly with another series of right- and left-handed whips.

Macho's nose came up to Calvin's stirrups. "You can't get by me," Calvin yelled to Robby, Macho's jockey. Rachel felt the pounding of Macho's hooves and dug in. She saw her challenger's eye, and she dug in some more, pinning her ears back, straining with every muscle, every fiber, every cell.

"She was never going to let Macho get by her," Calvin later said. "Every time he ran up to her, she dug in. . . . He ran up to me about three times in the lane and every time she gave me a little more run."

Rachel would not be denied, hitting the finish line a head in front.

Pandemonium reigned. People's emotions boiled over, rocking the historic grandstand like it had never been rocked before in its 160-year history. Several racing writers said they had never experienced postrace noise

Rachel gave it her all and held off Macho Again for the Woodward win. *Barbara Livingston*

levels as high as those in the stands after Rachel won the Woodward. It took Lisa Borel three days to recover her hearing. She had watched the race from the stands, though she couldn't see much through the crowd standing and cheering around her. She could, however, feel the Saratoga stands shaking after Rachel won. She was a little afraid the roof would collapse.

When Calvin and Rachel pulled up after the wire, Rachel's stride was gawky. She was winded and spent.

Calvin held his helmet above his head with both hands like it was a trophy.

Rachel was escorted back down the track by her trainer, assistant trainer, owners, and groom. They couldn't stop patting her shoulder, her neck, reliving the magic. It was a performance for the ages. Fans, handlers, owners, and trainers were all crying.

"She gutted it out," Calvin said to Jess as they gathered in the winner's circle.

"We never got to the bottom of her until the Woodward," says Calvin. "That was the only day I hit her. I had to grind her a bit."

Rachel had won but was not in her usual relaxed postrace condition. In the winner's circle her nostrils flared, her flanks heaved, her coat dripped with sweat and the cooling water sponged on by her grooms. Calvin placed the blanket of pink flowers over his shoulders and jumped from the saddle.

After the race several commentators tried to claim that Rachel had been racing against a mediocre field. But this was clearly untrue. Almost every horse entered the Woodward having won or placed second in a major stakes race. All had made their moves at Rachel at some point, and none ever ran as well again. This was a race that took every last effort Rachel had in her—it **gutted** her, and all those who challenged her.

Coming into the Woodward, Macho Again had won the Stephen Foster Handicap and New Orleans Handicap, as well as the previous year's Jim Dandy Stakes, and

Derby Trial Stakes with rousing stretch runs. He was second in the Preakness and Super Derby. He came into the Woodward off a fast-closing second to Bullsbay in the Whitney, run in a sharp 1:48 flat for the nine furlongs.

Bullsbay had won the Alysheba Stakes at Churchill Downs. In the Whitney, he exploded, going from 11 lengths back to the lead. His performance was one of the highlights of the meet.

After the Woodward, Macho Again and third-place finisher Bullsbay raced a total of 10 more times and managed only one second-place finish between them. Their careers were over.

Despite her early speed in the Woodward, Rachel had still been able to close her final eighth mile of that race in a respectable 12.48 seconds to complete the 1⅛ miles in 1:48.12, earning a 109 Beyer speed figure—this coming after a grueling campaign that saw her run a 108 Beyer in the Kentucky Oaks, a 108 in the Preakness, a 111 in the Mother Goose, and a monster 116 in the Haskell Invitational.

Ninety-seven-year-old racing legend John Nerud was at the Spa, as they call the Saratoga racetrack. He told reporters, "They . . . came after her one at a time and she put them all away. Those were tough older horses and they tried everything they could to get her beat and they couldn't. I think she's the best I've ever seen. I don't compare her to anyone."

Rachel's was the fastest Woodward time in the seven years it had been run at Saratoga Springs—faster than

Curlin, Quality Road, Lawyer Ron, Havre de Grace, Premium Tap, and To Honor and Serve.

What made her victory even more impressive was that it was her eighth of the year, at seven different racetracks, and ninth in succession, including victories over males in the Preakness and Haskell Invitational.

It was Rachel Alexandra's perseverance at the end of one of the most ambitious three-year-old campaigns in the history of the sport that truly defined her greatness and set off the wave of emotion that greeted her after the race and the pandemonium that engulfed all those standing on the racetrack. Exercise rider Dominic Terry wiped tears from behind his sunglasses. Steve buried his head in his wife's shoulder, crying like he never had before at the track.

Rachel Alexandra had become the first filly to win the Woodward. The last three-year-old filly to even run in the race was Summer Guest in 1972. This was the equivalent of a 23-year-old girl beating 30-something males. "The world's best athlete is a girl with four legs," one article proclaimed.

As they entered the winner's circle, Rachel and Calvin were cheered uproariously. Calvin traded his helmet for a black hat with RACHEL on it and spread the blanket of pink flowers on the horse's withers. They posed for photos. Cheering people crowded around them. "Rachel beat the boys!" one woman exclaimed over and over. Then Rachel walked back to her stable to enjoy some peace and quiet and some alfalfa. She had earned a rest.

The next morning, before dawn, she was sprawled in her stall when Steve came to start his day. He felt such a surge of pride and affection for her he wanted to hug her, but she sneered at him, as if to say, *Get away from me, you big sap.*

Horse of the Year

FOUR MONTHS AFTER Rachel's supersonic victory, chandeliers rattled as the volume in the Beverly Wilshire hotel ballroom rose to a dull roar. Hundreds of members of the American Thoroughbred horse racing establishment gathered to celebrate the year's best horses, trainers, breeders, and jockeys. Men with weathered faces and calloused hands wore black tie and women rocked floor-length evening gowns and diamonds as they milled about sipping wine and greeting old friends.

One dozen awards would be given out this evening, including the champion two-year-old and three-year-old of each gender, top breeder (Dolph was nominated), top jockey, and top owner. But in these Oscars of horse racing, the Best Picture award is Horse of the Year.

Only two horses, both fillies, as it turned out, were competing for Horse of the Year: Rachel Alexandra and Zenyatta. Zenyatta was a year older than Rachel, and although she was undefeated, she had run against females in four of her five races. (The Breeders Cup was the exception.) Rachel Alexandra showed her versatility by running more often (eight times), competing at more tracks, and defeating males at three different events.

Everyone took their seats, and dinner began. Jess sat at a big round table with Barbara and trainers Steve and Scott. Glasses tinkled, conversation was lively, and eyes were bright.

The awards began as dessert was being served. Jess and Barbara went up on stage to accept Rachel's trophy for Champion Three-Year-Old Filly. She won by a unanimous 232 votes. Shortly afterward, Zenyatta's owners, Jerry and Ann Moss, strode up onto the stage to accept their horse's trophy for Champion Older Female (231 votes). But who would win the coveted Horse of the Year crown?

Barbara and Jess knew that Rachel Alexandra had brought enormous joy and pleasure to racing fans everywhere. They knew she had run her best. They knew she had accomplished miracles. But they still wanted to win the award. How nice it would be to have that trophy on their mantelpiece, side by side with Curlin's Horse of the Year trophies from 2007 and 2008.

Before the president of the National Thoroughbred Racing Association (NTRA), Alex Waldrop, made the announcement, the crowd watched a short video clip of highlights from both Rachel's and Zenyatta's years. Although the two fillies had yet to meet on the racetrack, they were in a match race this evening.

After the video Alex acknowledged the people surrounding the horses. "Before I open the envelope I want you, one last time, to join to me in thanking the human connections of both of these outstanding athletes. Let's give them a round of applause."

The room exploded with applause, and soon the crowd was on its feet, giving the owners of the two fantastic fillies a rousing ovation. Then the room quieted. Alex opened the envelope. "The Eclipse Award for the 2009 Horse of the Year"—he paused—"is Rachel Alexandra."

Jess's face lit up. He and Barbara headed for the stage. With Barbara holding the trophy, Jess graciously acknowledged Zenyatta's achievements.

The 130-to-99 vote made Rachel the first three-year-old filly to be voted Horse of the Year since 1945. She was the first filly to win the Preakness Stakes since an era when flappers and Art Deco were popular, the first ever to win from the 13th gate—the farthest from the inside of the track—and the first filly to *ever* win the Woodward, beating older males.

Rachel Alexandra had made history over and over again. In a single year she had broken Ruffian's speed record and winning margin at the Mother Goose. She had beat the boys three times. At the Haskell she had

2009 Horse of the Year, Rachel Alexandra. *Jo Hooker*

won by the second-biggest margin and second-fastest time in the history of the race. Rachel Alexandra ruled the racetrack—and now she had the most prestigious racing award to prove it.

Rachel Retires

IN 2010 RACHEL RACED five times but struggled to regain her supersonic, light-footed form. Her trainers and owners agreed: it appeared her heart was no longer in the game. And so Jess, fully appreciating that Rachel had met and exceeded all challenges he had put before her, announced it was time for the fabulous filly to retire and begin the next chapter of her adventure.

Rachel traveled by horse van from Saratoga, where she had been training, to Stonestreet Farm in Lexington. Jess's home would now be Rachel's as well. The filly's life had come full circle: Stonestreet was next door to the farm where she was born, four years ago on that lonely January night when her mother rejected her—the farm where no one knew how great she would become.

In a tip of his hat to the winery business in which he had earned his fortune, Jess named each of his barns at Stonestreet for a kind of wine: Merlot, Zinfandel, Pinot

Rachel still had plenty of spunk, even in retirement.
Barbara Livingston

Grigio, Cabernet. The brick-paved barns are spacious, airy, and immaculate. For the first time since her days at Diamond D, Rachel walked out of her stall in the Cabernet barn into a covered area, not onto the asphalt and straw of the backside.

Rachel had to learn her new routine. With no regular workouts and now free to roam big, wide-open spaces unlike anything available at the racetrack, racehorses that come to retirement farms in **hot fit** form run like crazy. Sometimes equine managers sedate them a little bit so they don't hurt themselves, and it helps them slowly adjust to an easier pace of life. Hot Dixie Chick, Rachel's paddock mate, took almost two weeks to settle in.

First Rachel found herself in a small, round pen outside near her barn. She could run a bit in this pen without working up a head of steam, as she would if she were in a larger paddock. She seemed to understand almost immediately and settled right in.

Rachel and Hot Dixie Chick quickly became good friends. Dixie liked lying in the sun. Rachel would sometimes stand over her in a protective pose much like a mother and a foal. Dixie loved to roll on the ground, covering her coat in dirt and grass, but the only time Rachel got dirty was when she rubbed up against Dixie. Sometimes the two friends frolicked just like foals. And occasionally, when Rachel and Dixie came back to their barn, one or the other would have a hoof print on her chest.

Rachel greeting Calvin. *Lisa Borel*

Even though she adapted quickly to her new life, Rachel never forgot Calvin. When he came to the barn to visit her and called, "Big mama!" she came to the door of her stall, immediately lowered her ears and eyelids, and put her head right in Calvin's arms. She stayed like that for several long minutes, as if to say, *I missed you. Where have you been?*

Shortly after she retired, Rachel Alexandra was bred to Curlin, the two-time Horse of the Year that Jess also owned. Although Jess died before the foal was born, he lived long enough to know Rachel carried Curlin's foal. The 120-pound colt, nicknamed Taco, was born on the afternoon of Sunday, January 22, 2012. The bay foal splayed on the straw as his mother licked him and nuzzled him, his star blaze bright.

Rachel Alexandra was a natural mother, just like she had been a natural racehorse. As the only foal ever born of two Preakness and Woodward winners, Taco had the attention of the entire horse racing world. His birth was as noteworthy as his mother's was obscure.

Once he was strong enough, Taco—whose official name was Jess's Dream—and Rachel went to their

Rachel, here with her first foal, was a relaxed and natural mother.
Barbara Livingston

paddock, running some, resting some, and running again. Unlike most foals, Taco did not spend all his time tucked in by his mother's side. He liked to wander up to visitors to have his forehead rubbed or wander the paddock nosing in the grass, sniffing the air, or cavorting with Union Jackson, Hot Dixie Chick's foal.

Rachel seemed to take a cue from Taco and didn't fuss at him when he left her side. They seemed to have an affectionate bond built on mutual respect. Shortly after he was weaned, Taco moved to another farm in Versailles, Kentucky, to begin his training.

Taco tried to keep up with his record-setting mother.
Barbara Livingston

That spring Rachel was bred with Bernardini, another famous stallion, who won the Preakness and was named Champion Three-Year-Old Colt in 2006. This time, on February 12, 2013, at 2:30 AM, Rachel Alexandra gave birth to a very large, 140-pound filly, Rachel's Valentina. She was the largest foal born at Stonestreet that year. Rachel licked her baby clean as the foal struggled up from the straw on her toothpick legs to nurse. It looked like it was smooth sailing ahead.

But the day after she delivered her filly, Rachel Alexandra came within a whisker of death. She was rushed to the veterinarian. Part of her colon had been damaged during delivery, releasing bacteria into her abdominal cavity. She underwent six hours of surgery. Horses rarely, if ever, survive this kind of catastrophic emergency. Her filly was placed with a nurse mare, Ojos. They bonded immediately.

At midnight, surgery completed, technicians bedded Rachel down in a stall. They stayed with her, even lying next to her, until she could stand on all four legs. Once she came out of recovery, a vet technician named Brent Comer, who had come to love Rachel, stayed outside her stall, lucky number 13, for 15 hours every day.

Rachel cooperated completely as Brent and the other veterinarian staff members were doing everything they could to help her. It took many months before she was well enough to return home. As the trailer carrying her finally pulled up to Stonestreet, Rachel cried out as if to tell the other horses that she was home.

Rachel's recovery continued at Stonestreet. Brent stayed on, handwalking her every day, administering her medications, and grooming her. Although at first she was gentle and sweet, very soon she returned to her imperious ways and then some, trying to bite her handlers occasionally and needing a chain to handle her.

The first time she was turned out to the pasture, Rachel ripped around, rearing in the air, bucking, running, and playing. Alexandra the Great was back.

Acknowledgments

THIS BOOK WOULD NOT exist without the generosity, patience, and kindness of Hal and Renée Wiggins. Although the stories of Rachel I read in my newspaper excited me, I knew nothing at all about the world of Thoroughbred racing. They took me under their wings, explained so much about Thoroughbred racing and training, and vouched for me to everyone else in the racing world. They are so well respected and liked in the racing world that a word from them opened many doors that I do not think would have opened otherwise. Also whenever I felt myself lose momentum I would think about all the time they had given me, and I knew I could not give up.

Having said that, any mistakes there might be in this book are mine entirely.

I also want to thank Calvin and Lisa Borel, Jerry His-sam, Amy Kearns, Scott Blasi, Brett McClellan, Dede McGehee, Dolph and Ellen Morrison, and Scooter Dodwell for taking the time to speak with me. Photographers Suzie Hall, Barbara Livingston, Reed Palmer, and Bill Denver were endlessly patient with my frequent requests. And Keeneland librarian Betsy Baxter saved my bacon. Thank you, Betsy.

The Lexington, Kentucky, visitors bureau (VisitLEX) and my friends Cyndi Paceley, Karen Hewitt, and Stephanie Ceman all helped keep me going in various ways. As did my patient and supportive critique group. Thank you, Six Pens (in Pots)!

My deep thanks go also to my editors at Chicago Review Press: Lisa Reardon and Lindsey Schauer. Lisa believed in my book from the very beginning, included me in every step of the process, and kept me from being too repetitive. And my readers will never know all the mistakes Lindsey caught, sentence meanings she clarified, and punctuation she fixed, but they will benefit from her work nonetheless as they enjoy this book.

Thanks also to my family, all of whom have been my tireless boosters in all I have done. My daughter, Claire, gets a special mention for memorizing a really encouraging rejection letter and repeating it back to me whenever she saw my energy flagging.

Rachel's Record-Making Runs

IN THE COURSE OF HER three-year-old campaign, Rachel Alexandra became the first filly to defeat three classic-winning males and defeated the 1-2-3 finishers of the Kentucky Derby, the 1-2 finishers of the Whitney, the 1-2 finishers of the Stephen Foster, and the 1-3 finishers of the Belmont Stakes. Below is a summary of Rachel's finest races.

Fantasy Stakes Biggest margin in the history of the race.

Kentucky Oaks Biggest margin in the history of the race.

Preakness First filly to win the Preakness in 85 years and the first horse in history to win from post 13.

Mother Goose	Biggest margin in the history of the race, previously held by Ruffian, and fastest time in the history of the race.
Haskell	Second-biggest margin in the history of the race, second-fastest time in the history of the race by one-fifth of a second, and two-fifths of a second off the track record set by Spend a Buck 24 years ago.
Woodward	First filly in history to win the Woodward. Even winning the Woodward by a head and the Preakness by one length, her average margin of victory in 2009 was more than eight lengths.

Glossary

back stretch The long, straight part of a racetrack farthest away from the stands.

backside All the areas used by the stable employees, including the track kitchen, barns, dormitories where stable employees sleep, recreation area, and chapel.

blaze A distinguishing mark, typically white, that some horses have between the eyes.

bloodlines A horse's family history, a way to determine a horse's potential.

breeze Running on the track at about half or three-quarters of a horse's full speed. A light workout.

colostrum The first milk a mare gives to her foal; it is full of special nutrients.

dam A horse's mother.

damsire Maternal grandfather—the father of a horse's mother.

euthanized Humanely killed.

fetlock The lower part of a horse's leg, behind and above the hoof.

furlong One-eighth of a mile, a standard measure in Thoroughbred horse racing.

gallop A more relaxed stride than a breeze.

groom Someone whose job is to take care of the Thoroughbred's daily needs, such as feeding, watering, and walking.

gutted When a horse runs so hard it never runs at that level again in its career.

hand An old measure, now established as four inches, of a horse in hands from the ground to its withers, or top of the shoulder.

handwalk When a groom or stable hand walks a horse on a lead rather than having a rider on its back.

hobble Tie a short rope to a horse's two front legs to prevent it from walking.

hot fit A racehorse that has just retired and is still very fit and energetic.

hotwalker A person whose job it is to walk the horse around the shedrow after it races so it can cool down.

maiden A racehorse that has not won a race. Also, a mare that is having her first foal.

nurse mare A foster mother for a foal when a foal's biological mother can't take care of it.

overall track record The fastest time ever achieved at a certain racetrack, during any race run at that distance.

paddock A fenced open area, typically grassy.

purse The prize money paid to the winners, typically those finishing in first, second, and third places.

saddling paddock The area open to the public where racehorses gather before a race so people can assess their conditions.

sesamoid bone Two small bones above and at the back of the fetlock joint.

shank Rope or chain attached to a horse's bridle or halter that is used to lead the horse.

shark eye When a horse's eye shows a rim of white around the pupil.

shedrow Rows of barns at a track, including the overhangs in front of the barns.

sire The male parent of a horse.

splint An injury to the bone of the lower front leg.

tack The equipment needed to ride a racehorse—typically a saddle, a helmet, reins, goggles, and a saddle pad.

track pony A strong, steady horse, usually a quarter horse, that a track employee rides alongside each race horse to keep the racehorse steady on the track while not racing.

track record The fastest time achieved in the history of a specific race at a track.

Triple Crown A series of three races—the Kentucky Derby, the Preakness, and the Belmont—all run within six weeks of each other and at increasingly long distances.

Triple Tiara A series of three races—which vary from year to year—for fillies only, with races typically held the same weekends as the Triple Crown events.

weanling A horse just a few months old that has been weaned (stopped nursing) from its mother.

withers The part between a horse's neck and back; it is where a horse's height is measured from.

yearling A horse that is one year old.

Notes

All interviews cited were conducted by the author.

Chapter 1: A Nobody

"*Miss Dede, Lotta Kim is in labor*": Dede McGehee, interview, November 14, 2012.
"*If anything changes, let me know*": McGehee, interview.
"*Whoa, whoa, settle down*": McGehee, interview.

Chapter 2: Lotta B

"*Your little filly has an OCD*": Dolph Morrison, interview, October 17, 2012.

Chapter 3: Diamond D

"*Rachel can stay with me*": McGehee, interview; Morrison, interview.
"*Are you gonna fight me*": Scooter Dodwell, interview, November 8, 2012.

"*Lotta Kim was hard enough*": Dodwell, interview.
"*Good morning*": Dodwell, interview.
"*Look how long*": Dodwell, interview.
"*That's a girl*": Dodwell, interview.
"*Dolph wants to sell you*": Dodwell, interview.
"*We got a problem*": Dodwell, interview; Morrison, interview.
"*This filly is fast*": Dodwell, interview; Hal Wiggins, interview, July 9–10, 2012.

Chapter 4: Rocky Start

"*The big filly looks good*": H. Wiggins, interview; Brett McLellan, interview, December 13, 2012.
"*good airways*": D. Morrison, interview.
"*no menace, inside*": "Individual Horse Past Performances—Lifetime: Rachel Alexandra," *Daily Racing Form*, www1.drf.com /newsletter/RachelLifetime.pdf.
You big dummy: Renée Wiggins, interview, July 9, 2012.
"*You've been telling me*": R. Wiggins, interview.
"*Who is that?*": R. Wiggins, interview; Jo Hooker, interview, November 15, 2012.
"*Did you see*": H. Wiggins, interview.
"*Many horses would be half silly*": H. Wiggins, interview.
"*The only thing that gets Rachel*": H. Wiggins, interview.
"*Anyone can ride that horse*": McLellan, interview; H. Wiggins, interview.
"*I'm looking to sell*": Morrison, interview.

Chapter 5: Calvin on Board

"*He told me she just*": Lisa Borel, interview, November 27, 2015.
"*She looks like an incredible filly*": Calvin Borel, interview, November 16, 2012.
"*Breeze her five furlongs*": C. Borel, interview; Jerry Hissam, interview, November 16, 2012.
"*OK, big mama*": C. Borel, interview.
"*Looks like he likes your filly*": Hissam, interview.

"Mr. Hal, I'd like to ride": C. Borel, interview.

"I just worked the best horse": L. Borel, interview.

"You better bring a bucket": McLellan, interview.

"Whoa!": C. Borel, interview.

"This leader is finding more": Race video for the Golden Rod accessed from "Rachel Alexandra," *Blood-Horse*, www.bloodhorse.com /horse-racing/thoroughbred/rachel-alexandra/2006.

"Way to go": C. Borel, interview.

"When he won": L. Borel, interview.

"good, good horses": C. Borel, interview.

"If your filly runs": John Asher, interview, November 16, 2012; H. Wiggins, interview.

Chapter 6: The Martha Washington

"They're off!": Race video of the Martha Washington accessed from "Rachel Alexandra," *Blood-Horse*.

"I think you should take her": C. Borel, interview; H. Wiggins, interview.

You are the passenger: C. Borel, interview.

"Boss, I don't know": C. Borel, interview; H. Wiggins, interview.

"That was inexcusable": H. Wiggins, interview; Morrison, interview; C. Borel, interview; and McClellan, interview.

"She could run on asphalt": C. Borel, interview.

"Calvin, we were all concerned": C. Borel, interview; H. Wiggins, interview.

"I'm afraid we're": Mary Rampellini, "Rachel Alexandra Figures Too Tough," *Daily Racing Form*, April 5, 2009.

Chapter 7: Lead-up to the Kentucky Oaks

"Just take her out": H. Wiggins, interview.

"Five days out": C. Borel, interview; H. Wiggins, interview.

"more to calm": Jay Hovdey, "Two Fabulous Females Cross Paths," *Daily Racing Form*, May 1, 2009, www.drf.com/news /two-fabulous-females-cross-paths.

"Hal, here are some people": Asher, interview; H. Wiggins, interview.

"Good luck!": R. Wiggins, interview.
It's like I'm having: R. Wiggins, interview.
"If we win": H. Wiggins, interview.
"Make sure you're at": H. Wiggins, interview.
"Maybe if they made her": Jason Frakes, "Is Filly Rachel Alexandra Good Enough for Derby?," *Louisville (KY) Courier-Journal*, April 29, 2009.

Chapter 8: And They're Off!

"Rachel Alexandra is cruising": Race video for the Kentucky Oaks accessed from "Rachel Alexandra," *Blood-Horse.*
"I know she's a filly": Frakes, "Is Rachel Alexandra Good Enough?"
"I thought she had it": H. Wiggins, interview; R. Wiggins, interview.

Chapter 9: Kentucky Derby Surprise

Maybe I can get a check: C. Borel, interview.

Chapter 10: Rachel Sold

"I sold Rachel Alexandra": H. Wiggins, interview; R. Wiggins, interview; Morrison, interview.
"I want to buy your filly": Morrison, interview.
"crazy money": Morrison, interview.
"Hey, we had a lot of fun": H. Wiggins, interview.

Chapter 11: Calvin's Decision

"To be on the safe side": L. Borel, interview.
"Mr. Jackson, I'd love to ride": C. Borel, interview.
"Rachel means more": L. Borel, interview.
If we lose: C. Borel, interview.
"Listen, Calvin": C. Borel, interview; L. Borel, interview.

Chapter 12: The Preakness

"We are for sportsmanship": Joe Drape, "An Owner Clears a Filly's Preakness Path," *New York Times*, May 11, 2009.

"She might kick our butts": Jeff Lowe, "Rachel Alexandra Back in Preakness Mix After Controversy," *Thoroughbred Times Today*, May 11, 2009.

She's a racehorse: Scott Blasi, interview, August 21, 2013.

"Go get it done": C. Borel, interview.

Chapter 13: A Dazzling Display

"Mine That Bird tried": Race video for the Preakness accessed from "Rachel Alexandra," *Blood-Horse*.

"How good she really might": Jerry Bossert, "At Mother Goose Stakes, Rachel Alexandra Has Record-Setting Day," *New York Daily News*, June 28, 2009.

"She is capable": Bill Finley, "Rachel Alexandra Trying to Buck History," *New York Times*, May 16, 2009.

"We know she can run": George Vecsey, "Holding Her Own for Her New Team," *New York Times*, May 17, 2009.

"The filly has engaged": Joe Drape, "A Heart-Pounding Victory Catapults Filly into the Elite," *New York Times*, September 7, 2009.

Chapter 14: Rachel Fever

"She is a special filly": Mike Curry, "Rachel Dominant in Mother Goose," *Thoroughbred Times*, June 27, 2009.

"She's a great athlete": Curry, "Rachel Dominant."

"The Haskell changed everything": Bill Finley, "Rachel Has the Upper Hoof for Top Honor," ESPN, August 7, 2009, http://espn.go.com/sports/horse/columns/story?id=4384019&columnist=finley_bill.

Chapter 15: Will She Win the Woodward?

"Munnings looms": *Thoroughbred Daily News*, September 2, 2009.

"she was stronger": Dave Grening, "Rachel's Morning Chauffeur," *Daily Racing Form*, September 4, 2009.

"If they're talking": Jennie Rees, "Rachel Gets a Shot at the Big Boys: Will Face Older Males in Saturday's Woodward," *Louisville (KY) Courier-Journal*, September 1, 2009.

"She is being widely hailed": Andrew Beyer, "Rachel Alexandra Wins Woodward Stakes by a Head," *Washington Post*, September 6, 2009.

"It's OK": C. Borel, interview.

"There'll be no free ride": Race the Woodward accessed from "Rachel Alexandra," *Blood-Horse*.

"You can't get by me": C. Borel, interview.

"She was never going to": Bill Finley, "Rachel Alexandra Wins Woodward," *Lexington (KY) Herald-Leader*, September 6, 2009.

"She gutted it out": C. Borel, interview.

"We never got to the bottom": C. Borel, interview.

"They came after her": Steve Haskin, "Countdown to the Cup: Rachel Rocks the Spa," *Blood-Horse*, September 8, 2009, www.bloodhorse.com/horse-racing/articles/146837/countdown-to-the-cup-rachel-rocks-the-spa.

"I've never seen you crying": Haskin, "Countown."

"The world's best athlete": Drape, "Heart-Pounding Victory."

Chapter 16: Horse of the Year

"Before I open the envelope": "Rachel Alexandra 2009 Horse of the Year Announcement," YouTube video, 5:53, posted by "triplecrowndreamin," January 21, 2010, www.youtube.com/watch?v=xYT3e_d4rPU.

Bibliography

Blake, Denis. "Diamond in the Rough: Over the Past 25 Years Diamond D Ranch Has Laid the Groundwork for More Than 100 Stakes Winners." *Texas Thoroughbred*, November/December 2006.

Bossert, Jerry. "At Mother Goose Stakes, Rachel Alexandra Has Record-Setting Day." *New York Daily News*, June 28, 2009. www .nydailynews.com/sports/more-sports/mother-goose-stakes -rachel-alexandra-record-setting-day-article-1.378938.

Curry, Mike. "Rachel Alexandra Dominant in Mother Goose." *Thoroughbred Times.* June 27, 2009.

Doche, Marc. "The 10 Hottest Female Jockeys Scorching Race-tracks Around the Country." *Bleacher Report*, March 29, 2011. http://bleacherreport.com/articles/648654-the-10-hottest -female-jockeys-scorching-racetracks-around-the-country.

Drape, Joe. "An Owner Clears a Filly's Preakness Path." *New York Times*, May 11, 2009.

———. "Heart-Pounding Victory Catapults Filly into the Elite," *New York Times*, May 17, 2009.

Fidler, Katherine. "Bernardini Filly for Horse of the Year Alexandra." *Bloodstock*, February 13, 2013. http://bloodstock.racingpost.com/news/bloodstock/bernardini-filly-for-horse-of-the-year-alexandra/1203276.

Finley, Bill. "Filly Is a Champ, and May Not Be Finished." *New York Times*, May 16, 2009. www.nytimes.com/2009/05/17/sports/othersports/17preakness.html.

―――. "For the First Time at Saratoga, a Woman Is the Top Trainer." *New York Times*, May 8, 2009.

―――."Rachel Alexandra Trying to Buck History." *New York Times*, May 17, 2009.

―――. "Rachel Alexandra Wins Horse of the Year." *New York Times*, January 18, 2010. www.nytimes.com/2010/01/19/sports/19racing.html?ref=rachelalexandraracehorse.

―――. "Rachel Alexandra Wins Woodward." *Lexington (KY) Herald-Leader*, September 6, 2009.

Fish, Tim. "The House That Jess Jackson Built: The Family Behind California Wine Giant Kendall-Jackson Looks to the Future Without Its Founding Force." *Wine Spectator,* November 15, 2012. www.charmer-sunbelt.com/Premier/News%20and%20Events/Documents/WS%20Nov%202012.pdf.

Frakes, Jason. "Is Filly Rachel Alexandra Good Enough for Derby?" *Lexington (KY) Courier-Journal*, April 29, 2009.

―――. "Rachel Alexandra Romps by 20¼ Lengths." *Lexington (KY) Courier-Journal*, May 2, 2009.

Goldsmith, Liz. "Rachel Alexandra Is Home!" *Equine Ink* (blog), March 26, 2013. http://equineink.com/tag/rachel-alexandra.

Graves, Will. "Rachel Alexandra Almost a Certainty for Preakness." *Birmingham News*, 5/12/09.

Grening, David. "Rachel Alexandra Colt Name Announced: Jess's Dream." *Daily Racing Forum*, July 27,2012. www.drf.com/news/rachel-alexandra-colt-name-announced-jesss-dream.

―――. "Rachel's Morning Chauffeur." *Daily Racing Form*, September 2, 2009.

Haskin, Steve. "Calvin and Rachel: A Love Affair." *Hangin' with Haskin* (blog). *Blood-Horse*, March 31, 2016. http://cs.bloodhorse

.com/blogs/horse-racing-steve-haskin/archive/2016/03/31/calvin-and-rachel-a-love-affair.aspx.

———. "Commentary: Rachel Alexandra and Brent Comer: A Love Story," *Horse*, September 7, 2013. www.thehorse.com/articles/32504/commentary-rachel-alexandra-and-brent-comer-a-love-story.

———. "Countdown to the Cup: Rachel Rocks the Spa." *Blood-Horse*, September 8, 2009. www.bloodhorse.com/horse-racing/articles/146837/countdown-to-the-cup-rachel-rocks-the-spa.

———. "Countdown to the Cup: Three, Two, One . . . Phht." *Blood-Horse*, August 4, 2009. www.bloodhorse.com/horse-racing/articles/51958/countdown-to-the-cup-three-two-onephht#ixzz2ccgWqRnq.

———. "Haskin's Preakness Recap: Remarkable Rachel." *Blood-Horse*, May 18, 2009. www.bloodhorse.com/horse-racing/articles/50844/haskins-preakness-recap-remarkable-rachel#ixzz1r5lkYf2Z.

———. "The Rachel Experience: Rachel Alexandra's name can now be mentioned among the greats with her historic Woodward victory." *Blood-Horse*, September 12, 2009, 3274–3276.

———."Rachel Explanation Needed." *Hangin' with Haskin* (blog). *Blood-Horse*, September 29, 2010. http://cs.bloodhorse.com/blogs/horse-racing-steve-haskin/archive/2010/09/29/rachel-explanation-needed.aspx.

———. "Rachel Heads Field of Seven at Haskell." *Blood-Horse*, July 30, 2009. www.bloodhorse.com/horse-racing/articles/51901/rachel-heads-field-of-seven-in-haskell#ixzz2cchsxbFN.

———. "Rachel Rules: Rachel Alexandra Rips the Boys Again . . . This Time at the Haskell." *Blood-Horse*, August 8, 2009, 2814–2816.

Hoppert, Melissa, and Peter Blair. "Rachel Alexandra Wins the Preakness." *The Rail: The Race for the Triple Crown* (blog). *New York Times*, May 16, 2009. http://therail.blogs.nytimes.com/2009/05/16/live-from-the-134th-preakness-stakes/?_php=true&_type=blogs&_r=1.

Hoppert, Melissa. "Rachel Alexandra Has Almost No Competition." *New York Times*, June 27, 2009. www.nytimes .com/2009/06/28/sports/28racing.html?_r=0&pagewanted=all.

Layden, Tim. "The Gossip Girl." *Sports Illustrated*, December 7, 2009, 128–133.

———."Lady's First: Rachel Alexandra Proved Her Jockey Right by Wiring the Boys at the Preakness, but Not Without a Scare from Mine That Bird, Who Validated His Derby Victory." *Sports Illustrated*, May 25, 2009, 41–44.

Lowe, Jeff. "Rachel Alexandra Back in Preakness Mix After Controversy." *Thoroughbred Times Today*, May 11, 2009.

Liebman, Dan. "Borel Confident in Decision to Ride Filly." *Blood-Horse*, May 15, 2009. www.bloodhorse.com/horse-racing /articles/50788/borel-confident-in-decision-to-ride-filly#ixzz1r 5mnHMHZ.

Marr, Esther. "Lotta Heaven: Dr. Dede McGehee's Heaven Trees Farm Is Her Own Slice of Paradise." *Blood-Horse*, August 8, 2009, 2807–2811.

McGee, Marty. "A Day in the Life of Calvin Borel." ESPN, June 4, 2009. http://espn.go.com/sports/horse/triplecrown09/news /story?id=4231703.

McMillen, Gary. "Hal Wiggins: County Fair Trial Drew Trainer to Racing 43 Years Ago." *Backstretch*, March/April 2000, 112–17.

Mendoza, Sigi. "Understanding Thoroughbred Morning Workouts." *Lady and the Track*, December 1, 2014. www.ladyand thetrack.com/news/10630/understanding-thoroughbred -morning-workouts.html.

Mitchell, Ron. "The Day After: Still Raving About Rachel." *Blood-Horse*, May 17, 2009. www.bloodhorse.com/horse-racing /articles/50827/the-day-after-still-raving-about-rachel#ixzz1r 5mN9ysO.

Moody, Ralph. *Come On Seabiscuit!* Lincoln University of Nebraska Press, 1963.

Nack, William. *Ruffian: A Racetrack Romance*. New York: ESPN Books, 2007.

Oakford, Glenye Cain. "Rachel Alexandra, Foal 'Doing Well' Day After Birth." *Daily Racing Forum*, January 23, 2012. www.drf .com/news/rachel-alexandra-foal-doing-well-day-after-birth.

O'Brien, Keith. "Can a Woman Win the Derby?" *New York Times Magazine*, April 17, 2013. www.nytimes.com/2013/04/21 /magazine/can-rosie-napravnik-win-the-kentucky-derby .html?_r=0.

O'Meara, Brendan. *Six Weeks in Saratoga*. New York: State University of New York Press, 2011.

"Rachel Alexandra and Her Foal." *Through the Lens* (blog). *Blood-Horse*, February 17, 2012. http://cs.bloodhorse.com/blogs /throughthelens/archive/2012/02/17/rachel-alexandra-and-her -foal.aspx#sthash.ma7elrvz.dpuf.

"Rachel Alexandra Has Another Surgery." *Lexington (KY) Herald-Leader*, March 7, 2013. www.kentucky.com/2013/03/07/2547138 /more-surgery-for-rachel-alexandra.html.

"Rachel Wins NYRA 'Story of the Year.'" *Blood-Horse*, January 16, 2010. www.bloodhorse.com/horse-racing/articles/54844 /rachel-wins-nyra-story-of-the-year.

Rogers, Darren. "Jockey Calvin Borel Saluted Nov. 21–22 with Bobblehead Giveaway, Roast and More." Churchill Downs website, November 18, 2009. www.churchilldowns.com/news /archives/jockey-calvin-borel-saluted-nov-21-22-with-bobble head-giveaway-roast-more.

Scanlan, Lawrence. *The Big Red Horse: The Story of Secretariat and the Loyal Groom Who Loved Him*. Toronto: Harper Collins, 2007.

Schwartz, Jane. *Ruffian: Burning From the Start*. New York: Ballantine Books, 1994.

Shandler, Jason. "Rachel Holds Off Macho Again at Woodward." *Blood-Horse*, September 5, 2009. www.bloodhorse.com /horse-racing/articles/52440/rachel-holds-off-macho-again-in -woodward#ixzz1r5k0GduM.

Sheridan, Brock. "Rachel, Ruffian and the Amazon Roan." *The Brock Talk* (blog), September 29, 2010. http://thebrocktalk. blogspot.com/2010/09/rachel-ruffian-and-amazon-roan.html.

Shinar, Jack . "Off Track Doesn't Slow Rachel Alexandra." *Blood-Horse*, March 14, 2009. www.bloodhorse.com/horse-racing/articles/49662/off-track-doesnt-slow-rachel-alexandra.

Smith, Red. "Views of Sport." *American Experience*. PBS. www.pbs.org/wgbh/americanexperience/features/primary-resources/seabiscuits-obituary/.

Staff and Correspondents of *Blood-Horse* Publications. *Horse Racing Divas: From Azeri to Zenyatta, Twelve Fillies and Mares Who Achieved Racing's Highest Honor*. Lexington, KY: Eclipse Press, 2011.

Stewart, Julie June. "A Youthful Visit at Stonestreet Farm." *New York Times*, May 31, 2012.

Vecsey, George. "Holding Her Own for Her New Team." *New York Times*, May 17, 2009.

"Wiggins Talks Rachel." *Breeders Cup Chat* (blog). *Blood-Horse*. September 30, 2010. http://cs.bloodhorse.com/blogs/breeders-cup-chat/archive/2010/09/30/wiggins-talks-rachel.aspx.

Yates, Robert. "Rachel Alexandra Dominates Again." *Arkansas Democrat-Gazette*, April 6, 2009.

Yunt, Gary. "Rachel Alexandra Romps in 65th Running of the Golden Rod Stakes." Churchill Downs website. November 29, 2008. www.churchilldowns.com/news/archives/rachel-alexandra-romps-65th-running-golden-rod-stakes.

Zipse, Brian. "Remembering . . . Rachel Alexandra." *Zipse at the Track* (blog). *Horse Racing Nation*, January 29, 2016. www.horseracingnation.com/blogs/zatt/Remembering_Rachel_Alexandra_123.

Interviews

Asher, John (Churchill Downs public relations manager). November 16, 2012. Churchill Downs, KY.

Blasi, Scott (trainer). August 21, 2013. By phone.

Borel, Calvin (jockey). November 16, 2012. Churchill Downs, KY.

Borel, Lisa (wife of jockey Calvin Borel). November 27, 2015. By phone.

Dodwell, Scooter (runs Diamond D Ranch, where Rachel trained). January 8, 2012. By phone.

Hissam, Jerry (Calvin's agent). November 16, 2012. Churchill Downs, KY.

Kearns, Amy (Rachel's handler off the track). November 17, 2012. Stonestreet Farm, Lexington, KY.

McClellan, Brett (trainer). December 13, 2012. Hawthorne Racetrack, Chicago, IL.

McGehee, Dede (breeder on whose farm Rachel was born). November 15, 2012, Lexington, KY, including tour of farm.

Morrison, Dolph (breeder and owner). October 17, 2012, Columbia MO; November 15, 2012, Louisville, KY.

Wiggins, Hal (trainer). July 9–10, 2012; November 13–16, 2012; October 16, 2013. Houston, TX.

Wiggins, Renée (trainer Hal Wiggins' wife). July 9–10, 2012; November 13–16, 2012; October 16, 2013. Houston, TX.

Videos

Rachel's racing videos. "Rachel Alexandra." *Blood-Horse*. www.bloodhorse.com/horse-racing/thoroughbred/rachel-alexandra/2006.

Rachel's Story (about Hal befriending little Rachel through the Make-a-Wish Foundation). HorseRacing TV, February 10, 2012. www.tvg2.com/videos/inside-information-rachels-story.

The Secret Lives of Female Jockeys. Animal Planet. www.animalplanet.com/tv-shows/other/videos/secret-lives-of-female-jockeys.

"Rachel Alexandra in the Saratoga Winner's Circle." YouTube. Posted by "GoodGovDem," September 13, 2009. www.youtube.com/watch?v=LTEGEuMu9G8.

Index